Ferns of the Coastal Plain

Ferns

of the Coastal Plain

Their Lore, Legends and Uses

By Lin Dunbar
Illustrated by John Norton

University of South Carolina Press

Published in Columbia, South Carolina, by the
University of South Carolina Press

Manufactured in the United States of America

Front cover photo by Robert C. Clark

Library of Congress Cataloging-in-Publication Data

Dunbar, Lin.
    Ferns of the coastal plain : their lore, legends, and uses / by
Lin Dunbar.
        p.   cm.
    Bibliography: p.
    Includes index.
    ISBN 0-87249-594-9.   ISBN 0-87249-595-7 (pbk.)
    1. Ferns—Southern States—Identification. 2. Ferns—Southern
States—Folklore. 3. Ferns—Southern States—Utilization.
4. Coastal flora—Southern States—Identification. 5. Folklore—
Southern States. I. Title.
QK525.5.S7D85 1989
587'.3'0975—dc19   88-20646
                                                          CIP

To Dr. Richard D. Porcher

A sincere and heartfelt thank you for providing the spark that began a life's work filled with joy and wonder.

CALL TO SPRING

Aroused from their winter's slumber beneath
    trichome blankets,
Unfurling fiddleheads stretch sleepily
    in the spring sun.
Coiled extremities flex their lengths,
And grow with each expansion;
Until, fully alert from the exercise,
They take their proper place within
    the awakening forest.

Lin Dunbar

Contents

Illustrations

Note to the Reader

This book is arranged for easy identification of ferns in the field as well as for "armchair" enjoyment. Each fern is introduced and described with an accompanying illustration that highlights distinctive features of the sterile frond, fertile frond, and in many cases, growth pattern. The uses of the ferns and their associated folklore follow these descriptions. In this way, whether you are trying to identify a particular fern while in the field or relaxing at home, you will easily be able to locate the information needed. While cultivation tips are given for many of the fern species, collection of plants in federal or state parks is prohibited, and permission must be received from private landowners before taking plants. If you are interested in cultivating native ferns, please contact the many nurseries that specialize in wild plants.

I sincerely hope you will enjoy your fern forays and that you will gain a greater appreciation of the floristic world that is our heritage.

Acknowledgments

My love of ferns began with a suggestion by my botany professor, Dr. Richard Porcher, The Citadel, Charleston, S.C. He was updating the lists of plants found in the coastal counties of South Carolina and thought I might enjoy the fieldwork involved in cataloging the ferns found in this area. Not only did I enjoy the research, but my desire to learn more about our floristic heritage greatly increased and changed the course of my life's work. In addition, I am indebted to him for his encouragement and enthusiasm while working on the book, and for his generosity in taking the time from his very busy schedule and his own writing and teaching to read and critique the manuscript and to offer many valuable suggestions.

In the years and study that followed, another professor, Dr. John Rashford, anthropologist and ethnobotanist, College of Charleston, taught me an aspect of the relationship between man and plants interwoven in religion, myths, folklore, food production and subsistence. He initiated and encouraged an anthropological point of view that has intensified my curiosity and sense of wonder. My fields of study and interest have greatly broadened.

Though these two men, through their love of their own disciplines, infused me with the desire to learn more about plants and man and to write about my findings, they stand on the crest of the multitude of scientists, biologists, botanists, anthropologists, taxonomists, historians, folklorists, explorers, ethnographers and writers who have laid the groundwork from which today's scientific studies emerge. Without the painstaking work of these men and women, this book would not be possible. My bibliography lists many of these works, and by their inclusion I hope the authors will accept my sincerest appreciation.

I am most grateful to Dr. J. R. Massey, director of the Herbarium, University of North Carolina at Chapel Hill; Dr. John E. Fairey, III, director, Dr. Steven R. Hill, curator, and Dale Soblo, Clemson University Herbarium; Dr. David Lellinger, curator of ferns for the

U.S. National Herbarium, Smithsonian Institution; and Dr. Richard Porcher, for lending me a great number of herbarium specimens for illustration, and to The Citadel biology department for granting me access to the herbarium, files and records in the completion of this work.

In addition, I wish to acknowledge Dr. David Lellinger's tremendous assistance in reading, commenting and correcting the manuscript, and his help with the ferns of Virginia; Dr. A. Murray Evans, professor of botany, University of Tennessee, for his overview and suggestions for fern species listings and inclusion; Laura Mansberg, botanist, Alan Weakley, ecologist, of the North Carolina Natural Heritage Program, and Doug Rayner, botanist, South Carolina Wildlife and Marine Resources Department, for supplying me with current lists of ferns for those states.

I would also like to acknowledge the friendship and enthusiastic support of Dr. Maggie Pennington, professor of biology, College of Charleston, and to thank her for reading the manuscript, for her ideas and very helpful suggestions.

I am also very grateful to Greg Schmitt, professor of English, College of Charleston, for reading the manuscript and offering his encouragement, support, suggestions and grammatical skills.

Working with John Norton, this book's illustrator, has been a pleasure. Not only am I grateful for his accurate and aesthetically pleasing illustrations, but also for his caring, concern and interest taken in the project. I wish to thank him, too, for his many suggestions and ideas concerning the manuscript, layout and outline.

I am extremely grateful to the following people for their friendship and assistance: Morgan McClure for his invaluable assistance with insects, ideas, and resources; Pam Croen for her help in proofreading; the staff at the College of Charleston library, especially Veronique Aniel, Tom Gilson and Phil Powell; Tita Heins for her ghost story suggestions; Fran Donnelly, Françoise Boardman, Bruce Krucke, Dr. Paul Hamill; Dr. Paul Somers, botanist, Tennessee Department of Conservation; Albert E. Sanders, curator of natural sciences, Charleston Museum, for his assistance with moths; Warren Slesinger, editor, for his patience and kind suggestions; three companions who began the journey but are no longer with me; and especially my parents whose love and guidance have been an inspiration and a blessing.

I also owe a great debt of gratitude to my patient and generous husband, Henry, and my son, Michael, for their delightful company on field trips, their help in fixing meals as I worked and their tremendous support and encouragement throughout the project. No matter how often I got lost "in the weeds," they always found me and brought me home.

Ferns of the Coastal Plain

Introduction

There is something about being in a fern-filled shadowed woodland that reminds us of prehistoric forests, extinct mammals and a way of life we still don't fully understand. Perhaps it's the lush environment in which ferns are often found—along rippling streams, dappled trails, quiet swamps or cool dark forests—that fills us with an unexpected serenity. Or maybe it's the surprise we feel when we encounter vibrantly growing ferns in less plush conditions—the sandy pine barrens, high marshes and cracked brickwork.

The places ferns reside are as different and as wondrous as the ferns themselves. I have included various aspects of these plants (superstitions, folklore about the ferns and their habitats or common names, ghost stories and myths) to give a feeling of the interconnectedness of our world. These stories help us recognize that while this book is about the ferns that grow along the Coastal Plain, they are only a small part of the much greater web of life.

Fern Names

The need to name things is a valuable part of communication. In the field of science, accurate identification must be maintained. In order to have botanists and scientists share information and conduct research, everyone must understand the exact animal or plant being examined. Common names are just that—common to one locale or area. A fern commonly called "brake" in Virginia may be called "Huguenot" fern in South Carolina or "ladder" fern in Georgia. To ensure that everyone is speaking about the same plant, the International Code of Botanical Nomenclature was established to provide for uniformity in plant names. The *nomenclature* is the system of naming plants, animals, rocks or other objects. For plants, Latin or Latinized names are used.

In science, each plant name has two parts. The first, the *generic* name or *genus*, is often a noun that describes the plant, is the aboriginal name of the plant or is a name given in honor of a person. For instance, the generic name for "brake" fern is *Pteris*, meaning wing, and is a description of the frond.

The second part of the scientific name, the *specific epithet*, is usually an adjective or noun that frequently indicates either a particular characteristic of the plant or a name given in honor of an individual or in reference to the habitat of the particular plant. For the fern *Pteris multifida*, "multifida," the specific epithet, means many times cut, and alludes to the numerous leaflets of the fern.

Although taxonomists also place plants in a division, class, order and family, for purposes of this book we will be interested only in the genus and specific epithet.

The name that follows the scientific name is known as the *authority*, the person or persons who first named and described the plant. *Pteris multifida* L. indicates that this fern was first described by Carolus Linnaeus (the Latinized version of Carl Linné), an eighteenth-century Swedish naturalist. Though most scientific works abbreviate the name of the authority after the scientific name of the plant, I have instead spelled out the name of the individual for ease of reference.

As our knowledge of plants continues to grow, a plant first named and placed in a particular family may be found to have other characteristics (not at first realized) which would place that plant in a different branch of the taxonomic family. Another name is then given to the plant and the individual responsible for renaming the plant listed as the new authority. To ensure consistency and accuracy, the former authority is listed in parentheses: *Botrychium lunarioides* (Michaux) Swartz. In this example, Michaux was the first botanist to name the fern, but Swartz renamed and reclassified it at a later date. The plant, however, is the same.

Each of the ferns described in this book includes the scientific name, authority, as well as the common name(s). The common name is given here because it often describes the plant or lends an air of folklore or history. However, for purposes of accurate identification, especially when examining a fern's uses, the scientific name must be applied.

As with any field where new information is being discovered, the taxonomy of ferns is continually examined. For purposes of this work, however, nomenclature and descriptions are based on the *Manual of the Vascular Flora of the Carolinas*, by Albert E. Radford, Harry E. Ahles and C. Ritchie Bell (1968) and *A Field Manual of the Ferns & Fern-Allies of the United States and Canada* by David B. Lellinger (1985). County listings have been updated, and most fern specimens can be found in The Citadel Herbarium; the Clemson University Herbarium; the University of North Carolina Herbarium–Chapel Hill; and the U.S. National Herbarium, Smithsonian Institution, Washington, D.C.

Area Covered

Although many of the species listed in this book occur throughout the four states, the emphasis is on those ferns which grow in the Coastal Plain counties of Virginia, North Carolina, South Carolina and Georgia. A listing of specific counties can be found in the appendix. I have included those fern species that are most frequent or common in this region, and one or two rare ferns that are particularly interesting for their form, folklore or habitat. Most ferns that are either so rare or whose habitat the layman is unlikely to come across or those ferns that can only be identified as a separate species by the experts have not been included. For those interested, I urge you to check the bibliography for additional source materials.

Each of these four states consists of diverse habitats. Barrier islands, maritime forests, salt and fresh water marshes, bays, sandhills, bogs, swamps, limestone sinks, stream and river edges, rolling hills, pine, hardwood and mixed hardwood forests can all be found in this region. Plants will only grow where certain habitat requirements are met. If you are looking for a particular fern species, concentrate on its most typical habitat. However, while each fern species grows best in particular conditions, oftentimes a few "stragglers" or "adaptive" ferns will grow where one least expects. So while fern foraying, keep your eyes open. Nature is not static—and she will often surprise us.

1. Area covered

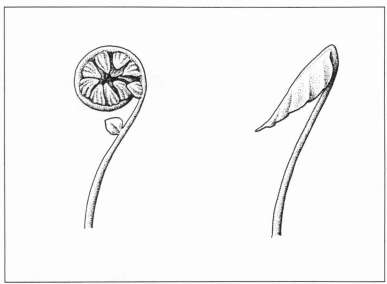

2. Fiddlehead and young frond of *Ophioglossum*

Fern Life Cycle and Reproduction

To the untrained eye, ferns look pretty much alike—all green foliage and no showy flowers to differentiate one plant from another. A closer look will reveal great differences in leaf shapes, fertile fronds and growth patterns.

Ferns grow from an underground stem called the *rhizome*. Its functions are storage of starch (food) for the plant, anchorage, the production of roots (which absorb minerals and water), and vegetative reproduction.

In the early stage of growth, the young fronds are tightly coiled and resemble the neck of a fiddle—hence the common name of *fiddlehead* or *crozier*. Yet for some species, as in *Ophioglossum* and *Botrychium*, the young fronds are not coiled but rather unfold as they emerge from the soil.

The part of the fern we are most familiar with is the *frond*. This is the part we see throughout the woods, along roadsides, often growing in moist soils. The frond consists of a *stipe* (also called *petiole*), containing the vascular tissues: the xylem which conducts

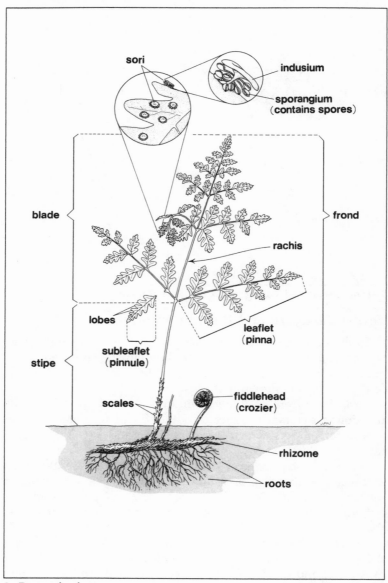

3. Parts of a fern

water and minerals from the rhizome and roots to the blade; and the phloem which conducts food throughout the plant.

The green tissue we think of as the leaf is called the *blade* (also called the *lamina*), and its function is to carry on photosynthesis. Typically, the blade is divided into smaller *leaflets* or *pinnae*, with even further divisions called *subleaflets* or *pinnules*. When these subleaflets are further divided, the green tissue is called a *lobe* and the blade is considered *bipinnate*. The arrangement, size and shape of the blade and its leaflets help to identify the particular fern species.

Ferns have two very different reproductive forms during the life cycle of one plant—the sexual, *gametophyte* or *prothallium* form and the asexual or *sporophyte* form. For many years, sexual reproduction of ferns and the role of sori in this process was not understood. This puzzle led to many superstitions, took over 150 years to completely comprehend, and yet can be summed up in three words: alternation of generations.

Ferns do not have flowers; on the back of certain blades or along the margins of the leaflets tiny *sori* develop. These structures have different shapes in different species: as beadlike structures, clusters of brown, roundish structures or even dustlike "lines" that follow the veins of the leaf or leaflet. In certain species, a flap of tissue, called an *indusium*, covers the sorus (singular for sori) while the sporangia and their spores develop. Depending on the specific species, these are variously formed into kidney, oval, round or umbrella shapes. These dark "spots" (inaccurately called fruitdots) have often been thought by the novice to be plant disease. In actuality, the sori are clusters of *sporangia* which produce the *spores*. Each single spore has the potential to develop a prothallium, the tiny sexual stage of the fern's life cycle. It is in this stage that sexual reproduction takes place.

When the spores are mature, the sporangia or capsules, through a drying and catapulting process, burst open and the spores are scattered in the wind. These dustlike spores are released from late spring through the fall, depending on the species. The wind can carry spores over long distances, but they must land on moist soil not only for germination into the prothallium stage, but also for the moisture necessary for sexual reproduction.

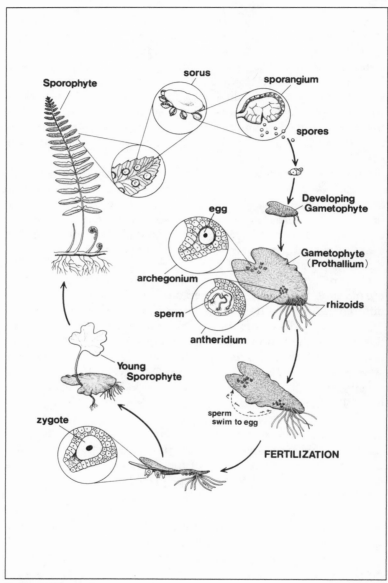

4. Fern life cycle

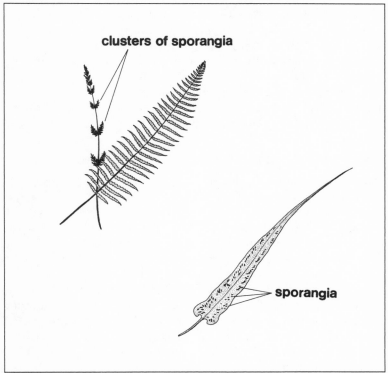

clusters of sporangia

sporangia

5. Sori on separate frond (*Osmunda cinnamomea*) and sori on same frond (*Asplenium rhizophyllum*)

When mature, the prothallium typically resembles a flat, heart-shaped structure without true roots or stems. This tiny form is often less than ¼ inch in diameter. The prothallium is anchored to the soil by *rhizoids*, rootlike filaments that help the plant absorb moisture and nutrients from the soil.

In addition to the rhizoids are two types of minute structures: the *antheridia*, or male reproductive structures, and the *archegonia*, or female reproductive structures. When the prothallium is bathed in moisture, the antheridia open and release the sperm cells into the water. Like protozoa, they "swim" through the water, propelling themselves via flagella until they reach the archegonia and fertilize the waiting egg cell. This sexual union of the sperm and egg cell results in a *zygote*, the beginning of the embryo that will develop into the sporophyte plant (asexual generation) of the fern. The young sporophyte will depend on the gametophyte until the new plant is able to produce its own food. Eventually, roots, an underground rhizome and leaves will develop, the prothallium will wither and die, and the characteristic fern will begin the process once again as it matures to produce sori.

Fern Identification and Key

While identifying plants without flowers may seem difficult at first, this book is designed to simplify the process. Species have been grouped according to the leaf shape of the sterile frond and number of divisions in the leaf blade. Ferns have been grouped: simple-leaved ferns; almost once-cut to once-cut ferns; almost twice-cut to twice-cut ferns; and almost thrice-cut to thrice-cut or lacy ferns.

Carefully study the fern to be identified. Decide how many divisions the sterile blade contains, and find the page number indicated for that particular leaf shape. Thumb through the illustrations until you see the fern similar to the one you wish to identify. Compare size, habitat, fertile frond and sori position for positive identification.

This book, however, cannot encompass all the variations and hybridizations that are currently being studied. For those wishing such information, a list of excellent field guides, manuals and journals is included in the bibliography.

By using the identification system presented here, the ferns found along the coastal region should be easily identified. There may be a few cases where hybridization or other variables makes even family identification uncertain. In these few cases, I suggest that the specimen be sent to a local university or extension service for positive identification.

Key

***Simple-Leaved Ferns** (Beginning on page 19.)*
Mosquito fern: *Azolla caroliniana*
Water spangles: *Salvinia minima*
Southern adder's tongue: *Ophioglossum pycnostichum*
Least adder's tongue: *Ophioglossum nudicaule*
Walking fern: *Asplenium rhizophyllum*

***Almost Once-Cut to Once-Cut Ferns** (Beginning on page 35.)*
Ebony spleenwort: *Asplenium platyneuron*
Blackstem spleenwort: *Asplenium resiliens*
Bicolored spleenwort: *Asplenium heterochroum*
Wagner's spleenwort: *Asplenium heteroresiliens*
Maidenhair spleenwort: *Asplenium trichomanes*
Hartford fern: *Lygodium palmatum*
Holly fern: *Cyrtomium falcatum*
Sensitive fern: *Onoclea sensibilis*
Purple cliff-brake: *Pellaea atropurpurea*
Resurrection fern: *Polypodium polypodioides*
Rock-cap fern: *Polypodium virginianum*
Golden polypody: *Polypodium aureum*
Christmas fern: *Polystichum acrostichoides*
Huguenot fern: *Pteris multifida*
Ladder brake: *Pteris vittata*
Netted chain fern: *Woodwardia areolata*

Almost Twice-Cut to Twice-Cut Ferns (Beginning on page 77.)
Southern lady fern: *Athyrium asplenioides*
Southern wood fern: *Dryopteris ludoviciana*
Crested wood fern: *Dryopteris cristata*
Log fern: *Dryopteris celsa*
Cinnamon fern: *Osmunda cinnamomea*
Interrupted fern: *Osmunda claytoniana*
Royal fern: *Osmunda regalis* var.
    spectabilis
Marsh fern: *Thelypteris palustris*
Widespread maiden fern: *Thelypteris
    kunthii*
Broad beech-fern: *Thelypteris hexagonoptera*
New York fern: *Thelypteris noveboracensis*
Downy maiden fern: *Thelypteris dentata*
Blunt-lobed woodsia: *Woodsia obtusa*
Virginia chain fern: *Woodwardia virginica*

Almost Thrice-Cut, Thrice-Cut or Lacy Ferns (Beginning on page 111.)
Southern maidenhair: *Adiantum
    capillus-veneris*
Northern maidenhair: *Adiantum
    pedatum*
Rattlesnake fern: *Botrychium virginianum*
Common grapefern: *Botrychium dissectum*
Southern grapefern: *Botrychium biternatum*
Moonwort: *Botrychium lunarioides*
Hay-scented fern: *Dennstaedtia punctilobula*
Evergreen wood fern: *Dryopteris intermedia*
Japanese climbing fern: *Lygodium japonicum*
Bracken: *Pteridium aquilinum*
Mariana maiden fern: *Thelypteris torresiana*

Fern Uses

Ferns are fascinating in their own right: they help bind the soil and prevent erosion, provide oxygen, form soil through the decay of old fronds, add beauty to the landscape and garden and larger species often provide shade that enables other plant species to grow.

Man has always used the plants around him for his sustenance and well being. Ferns, besides their role in garden landscaping and indoor decorating, have many other uses: animal fodder, thatching, food, medicine, fiber and dye. I have enumerated the uses of those ferns found in our area as well as how these particular species are used in other cultures. While this is not a complete list, my purpose is to show how one plant species, though important for its individuality, is also in its broadest sense a part of an entire web of life that spans region, state, nation and earth.

Fern Myths, Folklore and Symbolism

Man's natural instinct to explain phenomena through myth and legend extends to the world of ferns. The fact that ferns have neither flowers nor seeds puzzled the early observers and led to many superstitions. And not until the nineteenth century was the life cycle of the fern correctly explained.

In medieval times most people believed that fern "seeds" actually existed but were invisible. These invisible "seeds" were thought to impart to their owner certain magical powers such as opening locks and finding treasures, the ability to rule on earth, as well as the ability to ward off evil and defy the devil. Some legends tell us that fern "seed" was also a necessary ingredient in various love potions.

The Doctrine of Signatures that arose during this time combined medicine, astrology, botany and superstition. This theory asserted that nature had given particular shapes to leaves and flowers to help man determine the specific ailment the plant was intended to cure. For example, the heart-shaped leaf of a plant was thought to cure diseases of the heart; the root of the mandrake, shaped like a man, was supposedly useful as an aphrodisiac. So for plants like the ferns which distinctly grew and increased but had no visible reproductive organs, the conclusion was that one had only to learn to properly use the plant to become invisible.

Collection of "fern seed" was as important as the proper moment of its "blooming." Everything from special white sheets or white napkins placed under the ferns to the carrying of bibles, testaments and crosses was employed in the "seed's" collection. One procedure involved placing twelve pewter plates around the fern and waiting for the "seed" to pass the first eleven plates to finally rest on the twelfth. Another legend says the collector must be barefoot and in a religious state of mind while collecting; and yet another says that the person wishing to collect the fern "seed" be in the forest before midnight, find the fern, draw a circle around it and then pay no attention to the voices (the devil's or others) that he will hear. If this waiting individual turns his head toward the noises, he will never be able to turn it forward again. Yet another legend says that on the summer solstice, if one shoots an arrow at the sun when it is at its highest point in the sky, three drops of blood will fall. These will be the fern "seeds," and they will have magical powers such as those described above.

St. John's (Midsummer's) Eve was believed to be the best time for fern "seed" gathering. On this night, a fern would bloom with a golden blossom, and if a fortunate individual claimed the flower and then climbed a mountain with it in his hand, he would find gold. In Russia, too, the evening preceding St. John's Day was the one night to search for the fern "flower," for the "blossom" would only appear at midnight. The lucky person who witnessed this "flowering" would be granted anything he wished. In Russia, if the "golden flower" is plucked at midnight and tossed into the air, it will land over buried treasure. In Bohemia and Tyrol, fern "seed" is said to shine like gold. It possesses the magic of granting wishes, and the man or woman who carries fern "seed" in his pocket would be able to discover treasures. Many Bohemians also believe that by sprinkling fern "seed" over their savings the money will not decrease.

Fern "seed" is said to attract insect pests, yet it is considered a precious possession that can interpret the language of the fairies. In Swabia, the devil brings fern "seeds" between 11:00 P.M. and midnight on Christmas Eve. The bearer of this "seed" will then be able to do the work of twenty or thirty men, but must sell his soul to obtain the magical "seed."

This wide-spread belief in the wonders of fern "seed" was evident even in Shakespeare's time. In *Henry IV, Part I* the character Gadshill remarks: "We have the receipt of fern-seed, we walk invisible." To which his companion, Chamberlain, replies, "Nay, by my faith, I think you are more beholding to the night than to fern-seed for your walking invisible."

Closer to home, there are some Southerners who believe that fern "seed" in shoes will allow spirits to follow the bearer, while others believe that by sprinkling it around the house, the ghosts will stay away.

In addition to the fern "seeds," the fronds, too, attracted many myths and held such powers as driving the devil away, dissolving illusions, and protecting one from magical spells.

Long ago, the fiddleheads were called Lucky Hands or St. John's Hands and protected the possessor from sorcery and witches, but those who spoiled a fern plant would live the rest of their days with a confused mind. Fern leaves were hung over doors and windows to keep lightning away, and it was believed that a pregnant woman could suffer a miscarriage if she walked on any ferns.

The early Cherokee Indians used ferns in their treatment of rheumatism and heart troubles. Because ferns emerge from the earth in a coiled condition (fiddleheads) and later unfurl into a broad, flattened blade, the "uncurling properties" of a medicine made from this plant and taken properly, were believed to relieve the constriction of the arthritic or rheumatic limbs as well as heart troubles caused by the lungs wrapping "around it."

In other lands, a mattress or pillow stuffed with fern fronds was used to treat rheumatism, rickets and involuntary urination. And a "St. John's belt" was made by weaving fern fronds together and worn to cure any illness of the wearer.

In Cornish fairy mythology, ferns are associated with the Small Folk, or the inhabitants of ancient Cornwall. And in Poland when ferns are picked, a violent thunderstorm is supposed to result.

If a person takes a bite off the first fern seen in spring, that individual will not suffer from any toothaches all year and is supposedly protected from snake bites. In the Vosges Mountains, ferns were cut and burned on July 30 (feast of St. Abdon, the patron of hygiene), and the ashes believed to keep away unwanted guests and insects.

St. Patrick reputedly placed a curse on ferns (some think that is why ferns don't flower), yet the Irish use the fern as a symbol of fruitfulness, a tea substitute and a remedy for burns. A belief in Wales says that the person who wears a fern in his hat will lose his way and snakes will follow him wherever he goes. A cure for stomach aches is the fern found growing on a tree (probably a species of resurrection fern).

Ferns have also been used, like daisies, to tell if one is loved. A frond is picked and each leaflet plucked carries the words: "He loves me, he loves me not." Another superstition uses the same method to tell the occupation of one's husband: "Rich man, poor man, beggar, thief."

And even the sap from the fern stem had magical powers. When consumed, this liquid was believed to bless the taster with eternal youth.

Besides the use of myths and fables to help man explain the features of his world he didn't fully understand, people have also used symbols to represent other objects and as a way of saying more than is apparent. The use of symbolism entails an association between things often rich with meaning. Although each culture or locale may have its own set of symbols—the dove to Christians is a symbol of peace, while in other cultures the dove is often used in divination and love charms—the use of symbolism and its connotative meanings is worldwide. And ferns, too, have their own symbolic meanings.

George Ferguson in *Signs and Symbols in Christian Art* says, "Because the charm of this plant is seen only by the honest searcher, the fern symbolizes solitary humility, frankness and sincerity."*

---

* George Ferguson, *Signs and Symbols in Christian Art*. (New York: Oxford University Press, 1959) 36.

In English heraldry, the art or practice concerning coats of arms and genealogy, the fern was usually in the form of a fern-brake (see bracken fern) and was used in the family crest of Harter.

While the above represents general fern folklore, specific ferns are often associated with particular symbolic meanings, fables or lore; these will be discussed under those fern chapters.

Simple-Leaved Ferns

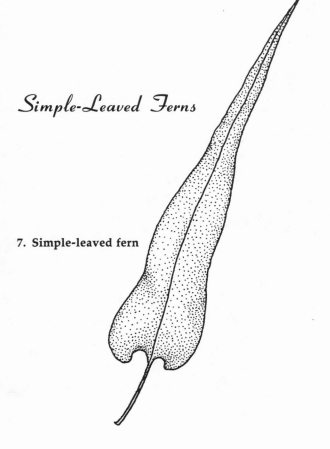

7. Simple-leaved fern

Azolla caroliniana **Willdenow**
Mosquito fern
Family: Azollaceae
(Virginia, North Carolina, South Carolina, Georgia)

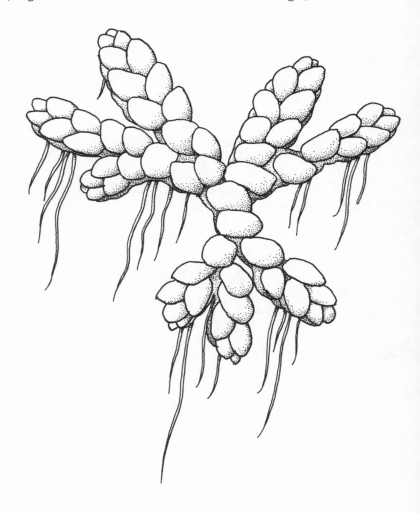

8. *Azolla caroliniana*/Mosquito fern

In the slow-moving streams and still ponds of the Coastal Plain, green to dark red plant-mats cover the surface of the water. A quick glance often mistakes this vegetation for algae or duckweed, but when more closely examined, the leaves lack the characteristic flat, roundish shape of duckweed and, instead, appear more erect and lobed. For as unusual as it may seem, these are the fronds of the tiny mosquito fern.

This aquatic plant is a mere ⅕ inch wide and ¼ inch long, with overlapping leaves in two rows, the larger leaf often submersed. In full sun, the mosquito fern assumes a reddish color, reminiscent of the Southern autumn. In its preferred shade habitat, the fern takes on a rich, bright green.

Fertile plants are not often found, but fern experts have pains-takingly observed and recorded the reproductive process of this aquatic plant, which for the most part takes place underwater. The sporangia are borne within a *sporocarp*, a multicellular structure formed by the fusion of the fertile frond's leaf margins. Sporocarps grow in pairs of two different sizes on the lobes of the lower leaf. The larger sporocarp is somewhat egg-shaped and filled with many *microsporangia* which contain the *microspores* (tiny male spores), while the smaller sporocarp is more roundish, like a globe, and bears a single *megasporangium* with only one *megaspore* (large female spore). Upon maturity, the sporocarp dehisces and sinks to the bottom of the pond or stream where, after a dormant period, the megaspores and microspores germinate. A series of cell divi-sions and various growth processes will occur until fertilization takes place (underwater), and the resulting embryo matures to produce several leaves and then floats to the water's surface.

An interesting aspect of the mosquito fern is its symbiotic asso-ciation with the blue-green alga, *Anabaena azollae*. This alga is found within the lobe of the emersed leaf (the leaf above the water) and is capable of fixing nitrogen. This means that the alga takes the gaseous nitrogen found in the air and converts it into a form that can be used beneficially by the fern as well as by other green plants. This is the equivalent of adding fertilizer to the soil. In Asian countries, particularly in the cultivation of rice, a different variety of mosquito fern is often used as a "green" manure. *Azolla* species have been used as a fertilizer for crops such as water bamboo, arrowhead and taro, the source of Hawaiian poi. Several varieties have been used as a fodder crop in Asia and parts of Africa and fed to pigs, ducks and chickens. And the plant has also been fried for human consumption.

Azolla's other uses include water purification, an ingredient in soap production by some African tribes, and in New Zealand, as a medicine to relieve sore throat.

Mosquito fern gets its common name from its growth pattern. The fern's habit of forming dense mats on the water's surface was thought to prevent mosquitos from laying eggs and their larvae from coming up for air. The fern's generic name, *Azolla,* is Greek and means "killed by drought" or "destroyed by drying" an allusion to the plant's need for an aquatic habitat.

Azolla reproduces fairly rapidly and is easily transplanted from one pond to another by birds. It grows well in circumneutral ponds and sluggish streams, and the fern has also been used in water gardens and aquaria.

Azolla caroliniana habitat

Salvinia minima Baker
Water Spangles
Family: Salviniaceae
(Georgia)

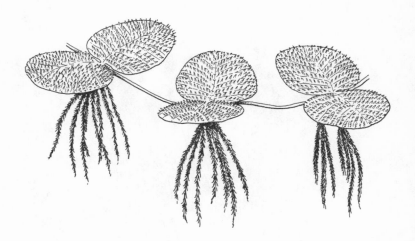

9. *Salvinia minima*/Water spangles

Floating on top of still ponds and waters, this fern looks like a mat of green sequins glittering on a woman's evening gown. *Salvinia minima* is just as its specific epithet implies—very, very small. The roundish, heart-shaped leaves are about ¼ inch in diameter. Leaves grow in pairs, and the upper surface of the leaves is covered with straw-colored hairs. Fertile fronds in this species (as in the other water-fern found in our area, *Azolla*) are called sporocarps, multicellular, cuplike structures formed on the submerged leaves. Both sporocarps—the one that produces the microspores (male) and the megaspore (female)—are the same size and shape and are born on trailing "roots" that are actually leaves.

Although this fern is more often found in Florida, it has been collected in a few counties of coastal Georgia. *Salvinia* grows in ponds, quiet waters and in marsh mud.

Ophioglossum pycnostichum (Fernald) Löve and Löve
Also known as: O. *vulgatum* var. *pycnostichum* Fernald

Southern adder's tongue; Adder's spit; Christ's spear

Family: Ophioglossaceae

(Virginia, North Carolina, South Carolina, Georgia)

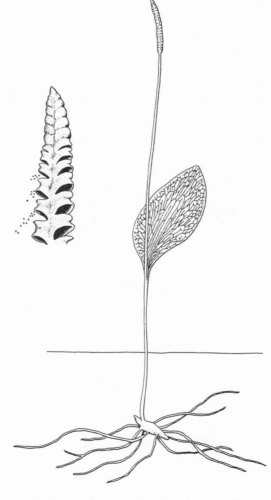

10. *Ophioglossum pycnostichum*/Southern adder's tongue

Between blades of grass and hiding under winter leaf litter, the Southern adder's tongue almost requires a hands-and-knees search. It's diminutive size—ranging from 3 to 12 inches—makes it easily overlooked among the taller green vegetation. For many years, adder's tongue was thought to be an uncommon fern, but this is not the case. Once the first plant is found, the eye seems to adjust to its distinguishing characteristics, and most people are able to locate many more specimens in the same area. The trick, however, is to find the first one.

The single, succulent, bright green, oval blade is held by a 2- to 5-inch stipe. The sterile blade is rounded with a tapering base, and has netted venation. The 1- to 9-inch stalk of the fertile frond arises near the base of the sterile blade and is topped with two rows of beadlike sporangia that appear to be embedded in the tissue.

Unlike the other terrestrial ferns, Southern adder's tongue (and all other species of *Ophioglossum*) does not have a woody, underground rhizome. Instead, the rootstock is fleshy and round. Another difference between other ferns and *Ophioglossum* and *Botrychium* is that these ferns do not have fiddleheads. While other ferns uncoil, these two fern types unfold laterally.

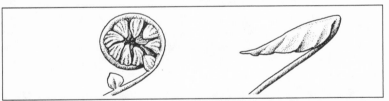

11. Coiled fiddlehead and young, unfolding succulent fern

Ophioglossum comes from the Greek *ophio*, meaning snake, and *glossus*, meaning tongue, which together allude to the appearance of the fertile frond within the sterile blade. The specific epithet, *pycnostichum*, means "with crowded rows" and refers to the placement of sporangia.

Man has always been mystified by snakes, and the fear of snakes and snakebite is common. A plant named for and associated with this reptile, then, bears some examination.

Snakes have long been venerated as well as abhorred and are used as a complex and universal symbol in almost every religious tradition. They have been associated with life and death, good and evil, dark and light and male and female.

Myth tells us that the adder's tongue was considered a magic plant and used in the pharmacopeia of witches along with other potent herbs and roots such as hemlock, henbane, mandrake, deadly nightshade, origanum, cypress, mistletoe and moonwort.

In the Doctrine of Signatures, the theory asserting that nature had given particular shapes to leaves and flowers to help man determine the illness the plant was intended to cure, the adder's tongue fern was seen as an antidote for snakebites.

Other herbalists found *Ophioglossum pycnostichum* valuable as a remedy for wounds. John Gerard, writing in the late 1500s, said of the Southern adder's tongue:

The leaves of Adder's tongue stamped in a stone mortar and boyled in Oile of Olive until the consumption of the juice, and until the herbe be dry and parched, and then strained, will yeeld a most excellent greene oyle, or balsame for green wounds [fresh or new wounds].*

Nicholas Culpepper, a seventeenth-century herbalist, found the juice of the fern useful when combined with horsetails (members of the plant kingdom belonging to the division Arthrophyta, of which only one genus, *Equisetum*, survives), for wounds of the breast, bowels or elsewhere, and to help stop vomiting or bleeding at the nose and mouth. The fern was also believed to help sore eyes and could be made into a green balsam for use with new as well as old wounds and ulcers and their associated swellings. The balsam was prepared by placing the fern leaves in oil, boiling or infusing the plant's properties into this medium, adding omphacine, or unripe olives and setting the mixture into the sun for several days. The blend would work even better if some clear turpentine were added.

Ophioglossum pycnostichum is found in the early spring, growing in moist, circumneutral soil, in floodplains, swamps, meadows and

---

* John Gerard, *The Herbal or General History of Plants*, [1633]. Rev. and enl. by Thomas Johnson. (New York: Dover Publications, 1975), 405.

grassy thickets, yet withers and dies by midsummer. Because it is difficult to cultivate, Southern adder's tongue is not recommended for the garden and is seldom seen outside its native habitat.

Ophioglossum nudicaule **Linnaeus**

Least adder's tongue; Slender adder's tongue

Family: Ophioglossaceae

(South Carolina, Georgia)

12. *Ophioglossum nudicaule*/Least adder's tongue

Another fern requiring a hands-and-knees search and sharp eyesight is *Ophioglossum nudicaule*. The common names of this fern, least or slender adder's tongue, refer to its petite size—1 to 4 inches—and its fragile look. The specific epithet, *nudicaule*, means "naked stem," a feature of the fern which probably adds to its diminutive appearance.

The oval-shaped blade, occasionally more than one, can sometimes appear oblong, has netted venation, and the fertile frond arises from the base of the blade.

Least adder's tongue grows in moist or low woodlands, sandy soils, lawns and fields. It is best located in early spring before it is obscured by other vegetation.

Asplenium rhizophyllum Linnaeus
Also known as: Camptosorus rhizophyllus (L.) Link

Walking fern

Family: Aspleniaceae

(Virginia, Georgia)

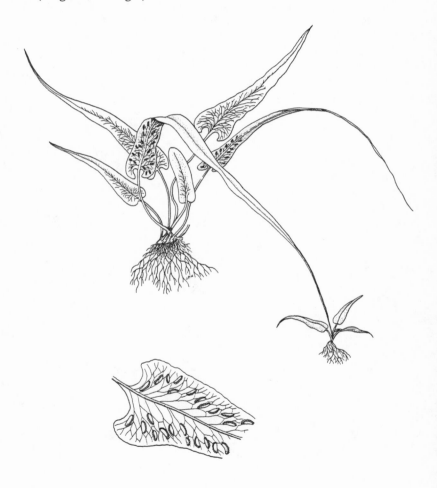

13. *Asplenium rhizophyllum*/**Walking fern**

Plants are one of nature's most immobile creations. Having neither legs nor wings, a tree or bush found in a particular location is pretty certain (barring man's interference, fire or flood) to be in that same place year after year. There is one fern, however, whose growth habits have inspired the common name "walking fern." This plant is *Asplenium rhizophyllum*, and it has the ability to root at the tips of the leaves and form new plants. (The specific epithet, *rhizophyllum*, refers to this characteristic.) The fronds typically arch away from the primary plant, and when the tips touch the ground, they will root and form new plants a small distance from the "parent" plant. These new ferns often create a circle around the original plant, giving the appearance of having "walked" from the primary plant outward.

The walking fern is evergreen with long, lance-shaped, entire to wavy-margined leaves, from 5 to almost 10 inches long, with eared or heart-shaped (auriculate) bases. Fertile fronds have scattered, linear sori covered with thin indusia.

Medicinally, the fern is astringent and mucilaginous, and the Cherokee Indians used the plant as an aid for swollen breasts. The entire plants of *A. rhizophyllum* and wild ginger (*Asarum canadense*) would be mixed with the roots and leaves of horse-balm (*Collinsonia canadensis*) to make a decoction, then applied to the swollen breast. In addition, the Cherokees drank the mixture to induce vomiting, which was thought to help the process.

Asplenium rhizophyllum grows in clusters on sheltered or moss-covered rocks or walls, especially limestone rocks, and is infrequent in the Coastal Plain. Taxonomists believe this fern to hybridize with *Asplenium montanum* to form *A. pinnatifidum* and with *A. platyneuron* to form *A. ebenoides* as well as to hybridize with several other *Aspleniums*.

Walking fern can be cultivated in moist soil to which limestone has been added and is especially attractive in rock gardens (perfect for rock crevices and pockets or between rocks) and in terraria.

Almost Once-Cut to Once-Cut Ferns

14. Almost once-cut

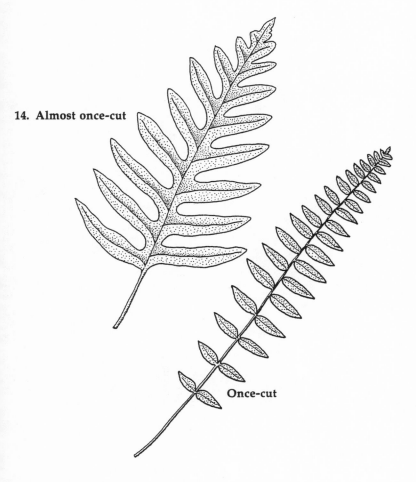

Once-cut

Asplenium platyneuron Linnaeus
Ebony spleenwort; Brownstem spleenwort
Family: Aspleniaceae

(Virginia, North Carolina, South Carolina, Georgia)

15. *Asplenium platyneuron*/Ebony spleenwort

The Coastal Plain is rich in evergreen plants, and the ebony spleenwort, *Asplenium platyneuron*, is one of them. Its shining dark brown stems prominently stand out through the undergrowth of fields and woods, and the fern often creates a soft silhouette against its familiar habitat—rocks and tree roots. Ebony spleenwort is considered a common fern in our area and grows well in pinelands, thickets and roadbanks as well as on masonry and rock walls.

Ebony spleenwort is a graceful fern, yet the brown-blackness and rigidity of its rachis creates a feeling of endurance and strength. Fronds are often twisted so that the blade faces the light.

Asplenium platyneuron is a medium-sized fern and grows in small colonies. It can reach a height of 18 inches, but because its fronds are slender and arching, the fern appears much smaller. Leaflets appear alternate on the rachis, are finely toothed and oblong in shape. The sterile fronds are recumbent and surround the erect fertile frond. Sori are also oblong, grow nearer the midvein than the margin and are covered with silvery, translucent indusia which wither upon maturity.

Asplenium, a Greek word meaning spleen, was named by Linnaeus in 1753. Some authorities claim the name comes from the shape of the leaflets, and others, like the sixteenth-century herbalist, Gerard, ascribe healing properties to a decoction of the fern in cases of enlarged spleens or obstructions of the spleen or liver. In Peru, however, the leaves of a related species are chewed for their flavor, which is said to be similar to coca.

Asplenium platyneuron can be grown in a fern garden or on the windowsill, though a soil rich in nutrients will kill the plant. The willowy, gently curving stipes also add a special enchantment to a hanging basket. In the garden, ebony spleenwort grows well in partial shade and moist, subacid soil.

Asplenium resiliens **Kunze**
Blackstem spleenwort
Family: Aspleniaceae
(North Carolina, South Carolina, Georgia)

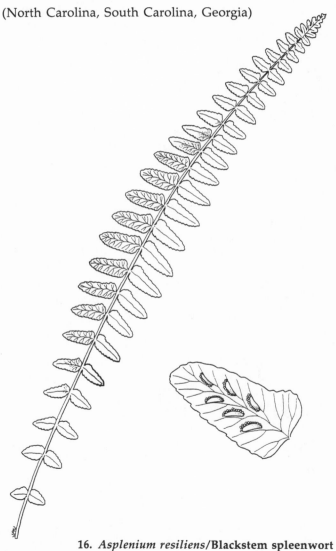

16. *Asplenium resiliens*/**Blackstem spleenwort**

Two other spleenworts that grow in the Coastal Plain, *Asplenium resiliens* and *Asplenium heteroresiliens*, are more difficult to find and are considered rare ferns. In South Carolina, blackstem spleenwort is considered a "threatened" species. *Asplenium resiliens*, or blackstem spleenwort, is smaller than *A. platyneuron*, and only reaches a height of 2 to 12 inches. The leaflets are evergreen, leathery, and opposite on the shiny black rachis. The margins are shallowly toothed and give the leaflet a wavy appearance. Fertile fronds have few sori, which are oblong in shape and covered by thin, laterally attached indusia.

This fern is found in small crevices of calcareous or limestone rocks, sinkholes and on shaded masonry.

Asplenium heterochroum Kunze
Bicolored spleenwort; Varicolored spleenwort
Family: Aspleniaceae
(Georgia)

17. *Asplenium heterochroum*/Bicolored spleenwort

This rock-loving fern gets its common name from the two colors of its stipe—black on the lower half and more brownish as it extends to the tip of the frond. The flattened stipe also has conspicuous green "wings" (expanded leaf tissue) which gives the fern another common name of varicolored spleenwort. Fronds grow from 3½ to almost 12 inches long and taper at both the tip and base of the blade. Leaflets are mostly opposite, with wavy-toothed margins and earlike projections on the upper margin nearest the rachis. As in the other spleenworts, the fertile fronds contain linear shaped, laterally attached indusia located more toward the midrib than the leaflet margins.

Asplenium heterochroum is found on calcareous rocks, limestone outcrops and sinkholes and is not cultivated. Taxonomists believe this species to hybridize with *A. resiliens* to form *A. heteroresiliens.*

Asplenium heteroresiliens Wagner
Wagner's spleenwort; Morzenti's spleenwort
Family: Aspleniaceae

(North Carolina, South Carolina, Georgia)

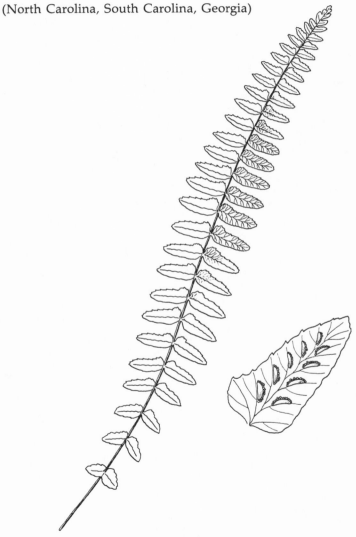

18. *Asplenium heteroresiliens*/Wagner's spleenwort

Asplenium heteroresiliens is similar in size and habitat to black-stem spleenwort, except that the leaflets are more sharply toothed and lobes appear only on the upper margin of the leaflet. It, too, is a small fern with fronds 3 to 10 inches long, and with opaque, green indusia on the fertile fronds.

This rare fern grows on soft limestone rocks and marl outcrops, and taxonomists believe this species to be a hybrid between *A. heterochroum* and *A. resiliens*. Distinguishing between *A. resiliens* and *A. heteroresiliens* is left to the experts who must count the number of chromosomes and distinguish between the shapes of the spores to be certain of species. However, *Asplenium heteroresiliens* has been determined to be a "nationally endangered" species which, though not listed on the federal register, is afforded a place on the list of plants by The Heritage Trust Program, which gives protection priority (the highest protection) for those species thus named.

When trying to distinguish between ebony, blackstem and Wagner's (Morzenti's) spleenworts, look first to see if the leaflets are alternate or opposite on the wiry, dark rachis. If they are alternate, you can be fairly confident you've got *platyneuron* or ebony spleenwort. If the leaflets are opposite and the habitat is limestone, you may have found one of the rare species. Since these ferns are uncommon, do not remove them from their environment. Instead, contact your local college, university or extension service so that a positive identification can be made.

Asplenium trichomanes Linnaeus
Maidenhair spleenwort
Family: Aspleniaceae

(Virginia)

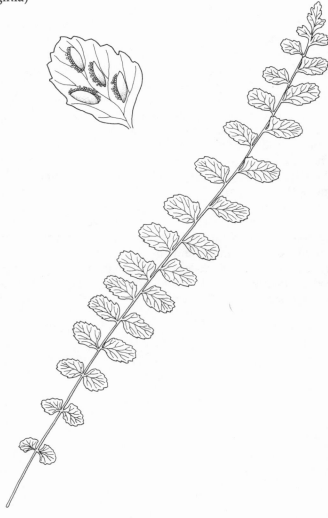

19. *Asplenium trichomanes*/Maidenhair spleenwort

Between moist, shaded crevices in calcareous rocks, the basal rosettes of *Asplenium trichomanes* form tufts of delicate, arching, evergreen fronds—rewarding the hiker and fern-seeker with its emerald beauty.

Maidenhair spleenwort is another small fern with fronds not often over 8 inches long and ½ inch wide. Tiny, roundish leaflets with entire to toothed margins grow opposite on the shiny, dark brown to purple rachis, becoming alternate toward the apex of the blade. Sori are few, linear shaped and covered with oblong indusia that usually disappear as sporangia mature. During the spring growing stage, older fronds die back, yet the entire frond is not lost. Instead, only the leaflets fall off the rachis and leave the thin, wiry rachises surrounding the new growth.

The term *trichomanes* refers to the delicateness of the fronds, yet the similarity in appearance between this fern and the Southern maidenhair, *Adiantum capillus-veneris*, gives its common name.

Maidenhair spleenwort is mucilaginous and astringent with a sweet smell when dry. It was substituted for *Adiantum capillus-veneris* in the preparation of Syrup of Capillaire and the fern was often used as a charm against witchcraft.

Though the plant is most often found on calcareous rocks and outcrops, maidenhair spleenwort also occurs in circumneutral to moderately acid soils. It is well suited for rock gardens where it can tolerate some sunlight and dry periods and grows best if limestone is added to the soil. Maidenhair spleenwort also makes a pretty plant for a hanging basket.

Lygodium palmatum (Bernhardi) Swartz
Hartford fern; American climbing fern; Climbing fern
Family: Schizaeaceae
(Virginia, North Carolina, South Carolina)

20. *Lygodium palmatum*/Hartford fern

In a quiet walk along a moist riverbank with sun-dappled shadows from tall trees and the heady scent of wildflowers, one can almost hear faint melodies wafting on the caressing breezes. The delicate, vinelike fern found here calls to mind fairy hands playing dainty harp strings. The Hartford fern, as it twines its way around and over its neighboring plants, has an ethereal, other-world quality.

From a creeping rhizome comes a shiny, brownish stipe fringed with small, light green leaflets. A single leaf can reach 2 to 4 feet in length with the sterile leaflets on the lower portion of the rachis and the fertile above. Sterile leaflets are alternate and fork into pairs of 2- to 6-inch, handlike subleaflets. Fertile leaflets are smaller than the sterile with oblong sori, covered by scalelike indusia, in a double row along the fingerlike segments.

The name Hartford fern comes from the plant's once common locality in Connecticut. This fern was so prized as an ornamental and so greatly collected that the Connecticut Legislature passed a law penalizing any individual found taking the fern from someone else's land. The specific epithet, *palmatum,* refers to the shape of the subleaflets—like the palm of a hand.

This fern is a native of Florida, but is not particularly common in our area. Hartford fern grows best in a northern climate, though the plant will lose its leaves with the winter frost. In the Southeast, this fern is most often found in the foothill and mountain regions, although several scattered collections have been made in the Coastal Plain.

Lygodium palmatum can be found in moist woodlands, wet thickets and swamps and in wet, sandy soil. It can be cultivated in moist, acid and humus-rich soil either in a garden protected from frost with plenty of support for its twining tendency or in an attractive hanging basket.

Cyrtomium falcatum **(Linnaeus) Presl**
Holly fern
Family: Dryopteridaceae
(South Carolina, Georgia)

21. *Cyrtomium falcatum*/Holly fern

During the Christmas season many homes are decorated with the green leaves and red berries of the holly tree. However, in the Coastal Plain, the holly fern, *Cyrtomium falcatum*, whose shiny, bright green leaflets bear a particular resemblance to the leaves of the holly tree, is often used in its place.

Cyrtomium is a Greek word meaning "cut in a curve and visible veins" and refers to the shape of the leaflet—gently curving to the apex—and the netlike arrangement of the fern's veins. The rhizome is erect and stout with dark brown scales that are also found along the stipe. Fronds can reach 11 to 24 inches tall and grow in a clustered arrangement that gives them the appearance of having been placed in an underground vase. Leaflets are alternate, leathery in texture, glossy and dark green. Though they look like holly tree leaves, they are not spiny.

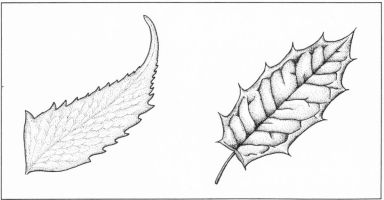

22. Holly fern leaflet and holly leaf

Fertile fronds are similar to the sterile, but have large, round sori covered by peltate indusia (attached from the center like an umbrella), scattered over the entire back side of the fertile leaflets.

In the Coastal Plain, holly fern is evergreen. The plant is native to parts of Asia. It escaped from cultivation and has become naturalized, meaning it can now be found growing in the wild.

Some authorities argue that this fern is similar enough to *Polystichum acrostichoides* to be placed within the same genus. Yet the scattered sori, as compared to the neatly rowed sori of the Christmas fern, and the netted venation differentiate the holly fern from *Polystichum*. However, in taxonomy, classifications are seldom final, and this genus may be changed in the future.

Holly ferns grow best in circumneutral soil but will invade masonry, rubble heaps and clay banks. They have been widely cultivated and used extensively in landscaping Coastal Plain gardens. Holly fern can also be kept as a potted plant provided the soil remains moist. A red ribbon tied around a pot of holly fern is a wonderful gift or table decoration for the holidays while the pleasure of this plant continues throughout the seasons.

Cyrtomium falcatum **growth pattern**

Onoclea sensibilis **Linnaeus**

Sensitive fern; Bead fern

Family: Woodsiaceae

(Virginia, North Carolina, South Carolina, Georgia)

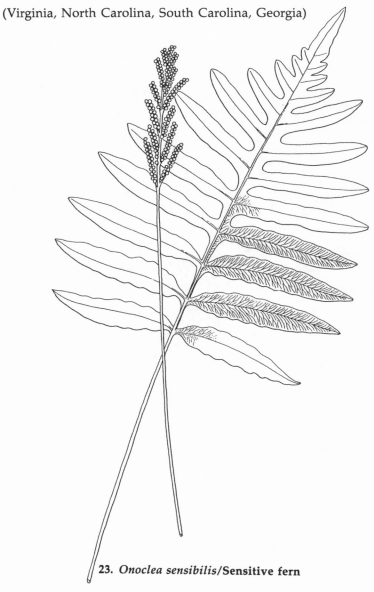

23. *Onoclea sensibilis*/**Sensitive fern**

Sensitive fern, *Onoclea sensibilis*, is a sturdy plant whose common name seems inappropriate when looking at its rich green color and vigorous growth pattern. The common name was most likely given to this fern because the sterile frond quickly dies with the first frost and leaves only the fertile spike standing through the winter months.

The rhizome is stout and creeping, and the spring fiddleheads have a pale red color. The broadly triangular fronds can reach a height of 31 inches, with veins that are prominent and netted. Leaflets appear opposite on the rachis and are winged at the axis with wavy margins (compare the alternate leaflets of *Woodwardia areolata*). Larger plants may have leaflets with indentions that are more deep than wavy.

Like *Woodwardia areolata*, the fertile frond is different than the sterile. The fertile frond of *Onoclea* is twice-divided with the segments rolling around the indusia-covered sori to form ball or grapelike structures that turn dark brown before the end of summer. *Onoclea* gets its common name of bead fern from the shape of these structures, which line up on only one side of the frond—giving the fertile frond a front and a back side. In addition, these structures help separate this fern from its sterile-leaved look-alike,

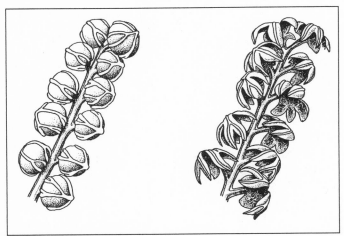

24. **Sporangia of** *Onoclea sensibilis* **closed and opened**

Woodwardia areolata. After the spore cases have opened and dispersed their brown spores, the fertile frond loses its round appearance and takes on a lacy look with opened segments resembling tiny hands.

Because of certain environmental conditions, leaf shapes can often appear different from the more familiar and recognized plant. Poison ivy (*Rhus radicans*), for example, has leaves that are extremely variable. While one recognizes the poison ivy leaf with entire margins growing in the sun, the same plant growing in the shade may produce wavy-edged or deeply lobed margins and may be easily mistaken for a different plant.

Studies have shown that the sterile frond of *Onoclea sensibilis* becomes variable occasionally; it may appear as though the frond was undecided on whether to remain sterile or become fertile. Sometimes some of the leaflets appear wavy-edged, while other leaflets on the same blade look as though the grape-shaped sori were about to burst through the leaf tissue. Some botanists have given this fern's occurrence a separate species, *obtusilobata*, though occurrence has more often been attributed to environmental conditions and kept as the same species, *sensibilis.*

This variable condition has also been reported occurring on *Osmunda cinnamomea*, cinnamon fern; *Polystichum acrostichoides*, Christmas fern; and *Woodwardia virginica*, Virginia chain fern, as well as ferns which do not grow in our area. Although exact causes have not been determined, environmental factors such as production of late fronds, increased shade, transplanting of the fern, late frosts, fire,

25. *Onoclea obtusilobata*

mowing, defoliation and plant injury have all been identified as possible reasons.

Onoclea sensibilis has been reported to be poisonous to horses when large amounts of the fern are consumed. Symptoms include incoordination, swelling of the liver and lesions in the nervous system and brain. Researchers have seen considerable variation in animal susceptibility and in the amount of fern provoking these symptoms.

Yet the rhizomes were used as food by the Iroquois Indians, and the sensitive fern borer moth, *Papaipema inquaesita*, finds this fern palatable as a food item for its larvae. This 1- to 1½-inch moth has a sharply angled median band that helps differentiate it from other similar-looking moths. Its front wings are light capucine yellow (yellow to pale orange) fading to a light auburn (coffee brown) on the wing's edges. Hind wings are pale yellow orange (light tan) with argus brown (chocolate brown) veins.* This species does not have any spots on the front wings. Sightings of this moth usually occur in September and October.

Onoclea sensibilis does well in sun or shade, moderately damp acid soils, muddy ditches, marshes, seepage areas and swamps. Since it tends to be invasive and take over more delicate plants, sensitive fern is not recommended for home gardens.

26. *Papaipema inquaesita*/**Sensitive fern borer moth**

---

* Colors are keyed to Robert Ridgway. *Color Standards and Color Nomenclature.* Washington, D.C., 1912. Colors in parentheses are descriptive.

Pellaea atropurpurea (Linnaeus) Link
Purple cliff-brake
Family: Adiantaceae (Pteridaceae)

(Virginia, North Carolina)

As some tall cliff that lifts its awful form,
Swells from the vale, and midway leaves the storm,—
Though round its breast the rolling clouds are spread
Eternal sunshine settles on its head.
—Oliver Goldsmith
The Deserted Village

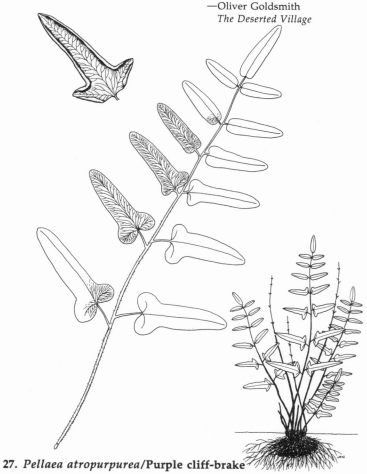

27. *Pellaea atropurpurea*/**Purple cliff-brake**

In the Southeast, the purple cliff-brake most often occupies rocky, hard-to-get-at cliff ridges found in the mountains; however, the limestone outcrops that freckle the coastal region will occasionally maintain a colony of this striking fern. *Pellaea atropurpurea* is a somewhat small plant—only 7 to 20 inches tall. The short-creeping rhizome produces leathery, evergreen sterile fronds with widely spaced, almost opposite leaflets. Though the leaflets are mostly linear in shape, some leaflets will have an extended lobe at their base, or the lobe will be completely cut and will create the look of a compound leaf. The specific epithet, *atropurpurea*, means "dark purple" and refers to the fern's most recognizable characteristic, the hairy, dark purple-brown stipes. Against the backdrop of rocks or other vegetation, the color of the stipes is a sure indication of the purple cliff-brake.

The fertile fronds are notable, too. The sori line the leaf margins in such a way as to almost create a dark brown outline on the underside of the leaflet. Sori have no true indusia, but the leaf margins roll over the maturing sporangia in the fashion of a "false" indusia.

Medicinally, a tea was made from this fern by some of the western American Indian tribes and used to flush the kidneys and tone the blood. It was also drunk in the summer to prevent sunstroke.

Purple cliff-brake grows in dry conditions on rocky cliffs, limestone outcrops and occasionally on masonry walls. It can be cultivated in a flowerpot or rock garden. *Pellaea atropurpurea* will tolerate some sun and does best if the soil is kept on the dry side.

Polypodium polypodioides (Linnaeus) Watt
Resurrection fern; Gray polypody
Family: Polypodiaceae
(Virginia, North Carolina, South Carolina, Georgia)

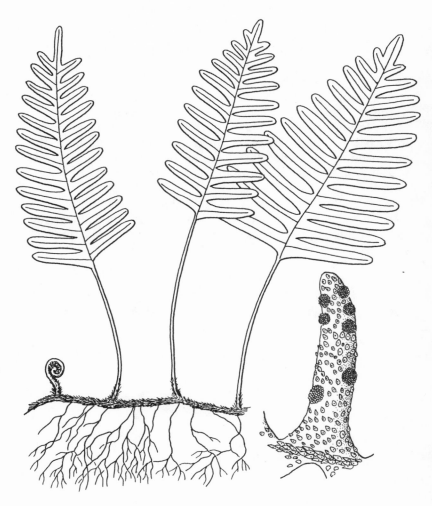

28. *Polypodium polypodioides*/Resurrection fern

Along the meandering roads of the Coastal Plain, massive live oaks drip with gray Spanish moss beards—often forming deep green, living tunnels that arch over the narrow roadways. Rippling from the sprawling limbs and sturdy trunks of these aging giants are cascades of resurrection fern, *Polypodium polypodioides*.

Resurrection fern is a small evergreen plant, only 5 to 7 inches tall. The oval blade is dark green above, brownish beneath, and the leaflets appear alternate on the rachis. Fertile blades have medium- to large-sized round sori without indusia, which are orange at first and turn brown upon maturity. Sori appear near the margins of the leaflets and are so deeply embedded in the blade that they frequently form small bumps on the top surface of the leaflets. The spore cases are difficult to see, however, because of the many scales surrounding them. The sterile fronds of its cousin, *Polypodium virginianum*, look similar, but one distinguishing feature of the resurrection fern is the tiny, dark, hairlike scales on the stipe and blade. In contrast, the stipes of the rock-cap fern (*P. virginianum*) are smooth and do not have these "hairs."

After a period of drought, you can easily mistake the resurrection fern, now gray, shriveled and looking like scaling tree bark, for dead. Given sufficient moisture, however, the withered look disappears, and the leathery, verdant fern returns to life. This ability, to adapt to arid conditions and then return to luxuriance, gives resurrection fern its common name.

The scientific name, *polypodium*, was given to this plant by Linnaeus and means "many feet," alluding either to the scars left by old stipes on the rhizome or the way the

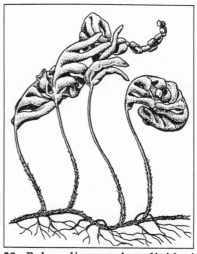

29. *Polypodium polypodioides/* **dried fronds**

fern's scaly rhizome seems to "walk" or creep over its host plant, most often an oak tree.

Oaks have been revered throughout history, and those plants which grew on these trees often became associated with their mystery and veneration. All species of oaks were considered a symbol of strength and courage and became one of the most widely worshiped trees. Perhaps the best known oak worshippers were the Celtic druids, so named for the tree itself. Not only did Druids worship these trees, but they also honored all things associated with or growing on the oak, such as mistletoe and fern.

Oak worshippers and medieval people gave wondrous properties to the fern "seeds" of these magical oak-growing ferns. These elusive "seeds" were said to bloom like fire or gold on Midsummer's Eve. When held, the "seeds" enabled their possessor to find hidden treasure. And if fern "seed" were mixed with money in one's pocket, the wealth would never decrease, no matter how much was spent.

Resurrection fern is used medicinally in Central America to benefit the blood; lower blood pressure; as a remedy for liver ailments; to relieve hoarseness, coughs and fevers, and to strengthen the heart.

Polypodium polypodioides is commonly found anchored to the rough bark of trees and is considered an epiphyte: *epi* meaning upon and *phyte* meaning plant. Though it lives on its host plant, resurrection fern does not derive any food or nutrients from it—the fern simply uses the host plant for physical support.

Besides various oaks, resurrection fern forms colonies on many other species of rough-barked, hardwood trees such as cedar, apple, pecan and elm, and grows well near or on moist, shaded rock surfaces. The fern is occasionally found in acid to circumneutral soil, on rotten wood and sometimes in the damp and shaded cracks of brickwork.

Polypodium polypodioides can be cultivated in moist circumneutral potting soil in partial sun and is perfect for rock gardens. In addition, its diminutive size makes it a good companion plant for terraria.

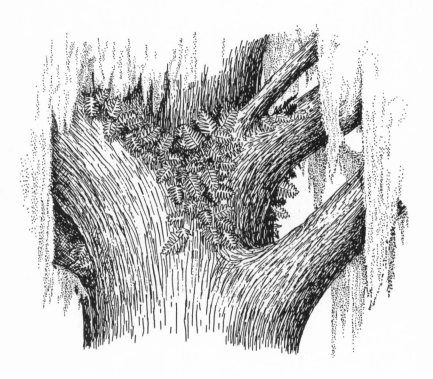

Polypodium polypodioides **growth pattern**

Polypodium virginianum Linnaeus
Also known as: **Polypodium vulgare** Linnaeus

Rock-cap fern; Virginia polypod; Common polypody; Sweet fern

Family: Polypodiaceae

(Virginia, North Carolina)

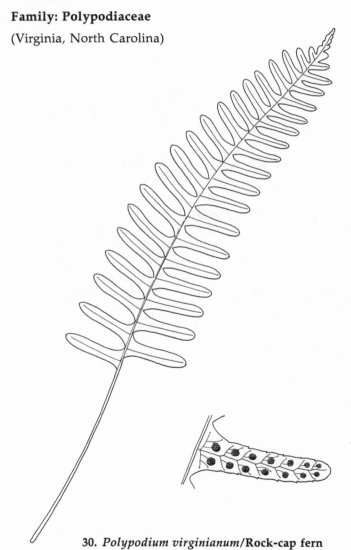

30. *Polypodium virginianum*/Rock-cap fern

The term *Coastal Plain* often brings to mind vistas of wide, sandy beaches, dune grasses and swaying palmettos. Other times, the term *Coastal Plain* creates images of deeply shadowed and watery swamps, winding rivers and gentle, rippling streams. Yet the region is favored with a number of varied habitats, which dot the landscape with rocky ledges, cliffs and boulders. Although these sites are somewhat infrequent, when they do occur, as they do in Virginia and North Carolina, the evergreen rock-cap fern, *Polypodium virginianum,* is very often found forming dense mats on the dry to moist, shaded rock surfaces.

Like its cousin, the resurrection fern, the rock-cap fern is tiny— from 3½ to 13½ inches tall. Its rhizome is creeping and covered with brown scales. Unlike the resurrection fern, which is "scaly," the stipe and leaflets of rock-cap fern are smooth and without scales. The oblong blade is dark green, often with a golden tint, leathery in texture and divided into 11 to 18 pairs of leaflets. Large, round sori without indusia are found in one row on each side of the midvein on the upper lobes of the fertile fronds. When immature, the sori are greenish white and later turn red-brown.

The rock-cap fern has been used medicinally since ancient times. The root has been used as a purgative (in the form of a very strong tea) for worms and in weaker doses as a tonic, laxative and expectorant. It was useful for coughs, hoarseness, consumption and other respiratory problems, loss of appetite, fever and jaundice. Rock-cap fern has been made into a wash for external wounds and for skin diseases. Nicholas Culpepper, a seventeenth-century herbalist, recommended this fern for those with melancholy or fever, hardness of the spleen, colic and troublesome sleep. He suggested that the dried roots be mixed with honey and applied externally to those body parts out of joint as well as to the nose to cure "polypus" (the disease where polyps or abnormal tissue growths develop in organs or structures such as the nose). Culpepper also suggested a broth of rock-cap fern, beets, mallow, parsley, cumin, ginger, fennel and anise for use as a mild purgative.

In Europe the rhizome of the rock-cap fern was used to flavor liqueurs, as an emollient, and when combined with digitalis, to treat epilepsy. In Switzerland the rhizome was used for respiratory ailments. A decoction of rock-cap fern rhizome and fir needles was used in India to treat measles, and when roasted, the rhizome was chewed to relieve coughs.

Today, herbal remedy practitioners seem to concur with several of these "old-fashioned" uses. A decoction of the root (the dried or fresh root is boiled and the "tea" sweetened with honey) has been found useful as a laxative, digestive tonic, appetite stimulant and to help relieve coughs and respiratory ailments.

As a different benefit, the ashes of this fern, as well as those of bracken, contain a large amount of potash and so were used in the manufacture of glass.

Although rock-cap fern is occasionally found growing on old stumps, logs and in rock crevices, it rarely grows on tree trunks like its cousin, resurrection fern, and can be found in circumneutral soil on rocks and ledges. *Polypodium virginianum* is easy to cultivate in shady, damp (not too wet) soil, and it makes an attractive addition to a rock garden. For indoor planting, rock-cap fern is ideal for terraria.

Polypodium virginianum habitat

Polypodium aureum **Linnaeus**
  Also known as: *Phelebodium aureum* **Linnaeus**

Golden polypody; Goldfoot fern; Rabbitfoot fern

Family: Polypodiaceae

(Georgia)

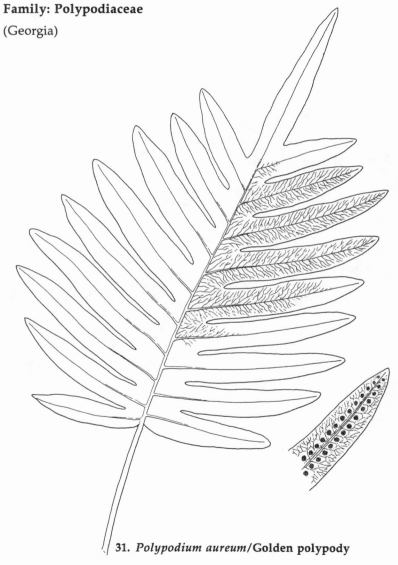

31. *Polypodium aureum*/**Golden polypody**

While the two other species of *Polypodium* found in the Coastal Plain are rather diminutive, fronds of the golden polypody are substantially larger—from 15 to 35 inches long. The blue-green blade, which later turns a yellow-green color, is divided into four to nine pairs of leaflets ranging from ¾ to 1¾ inches wide with one oblong-shaped leaflet terminating the tip of the frond. Sori are large, round, without indusia and grow in two rows along the midvein of the leaflets.

Golden polypody has a creeping rhizome, about ½ inch thick, quite stockier than its area cousins, which is covered with reddish-orange scales. Because of the color of these hairy scales, Linnaeus named the fern golden polypody. The thickness of the rhizome covered by these "hairs" also gives the fern the look of an animal's foot and another of its common names—rabbit's foot fern. (The cultivated rabbit's foot ferns, however, are usually species of *Davallia*.)

Golden polypody is abundant in the Florida-Central America region and is used extensively in this region as a panacea. Decoctions are often administered for kidney complaints, to relieve hypertension, for internal tumors, to relieve asthma and for lung and heart ailments. In addition, the fern is used to treat hoarseness, respiratory problems and to stop hemorrhages.

Golden polypody is epiphytic and grows on the crowns of palmetto trees (*Sabal palmetto*), on the rough bark of oaks and on crumbly limestone. It makes a beautiful cultivated plant, and as the fronds usually arch, golden polypody is especially attractive in hanging baskets. A mixture of sphagnum moss, humus and sand works well. *Polypodium aureum* can tolerate some sunlight. It grows best if kept moist.

Polystichum acrostichoides (Michaux) Schott
Christmas fern
Family: Dryopteridaceae (Aspidiaceae)

(Virginia, North Carolina, South Carolina, Georgia)

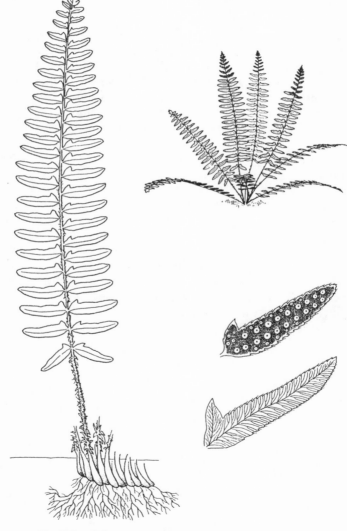

32. *Polystichum acrostichoides*/Christmas fern

During the winter season when most tree limbs are bare and when brown seems to be the prevalent color, the Coastal Plain landscape is spotted with an abundance of evergreen foliage. Green dresses the pines, magnolias, palmettos and live oaks, while on the ground two ferns remain vibrant, their names matching the holiday season: Christmas fern and holly fern.

Polystichum acrostichoides receives its common name of Christmas fern from the shape of the leaflet—the prominent "ear" on each helps create a resemblance to Santa's sleigh or when held vertically, a Christmas stocking—and from the fact that the fronds remain green at Christmas. Actually, the word *Polystichum* is Greek for many rows—a reference to the way the sori line the fertile fronds.

Christmas fern grows in bouquetlike clusters from a central stout and scaly rhizome. Fiddleheads are covered with shiny, silvery gray-white scales that stand out strikingly against the dark green foliage. Fronds can reach a height of 28 inches, with the sterile fronds somewhat prostrate, short and broad, and the fertile fronds more erect, taller, thinner, and the leaflets smaller toward the apex. Leaves are evergreen and remain shiny and lustrous throughout our winters.

Leaflets are alternate on the brown, scaly rachis, have bristle-toothed, holly-like edges and a prominent "ear" or lobe near the stalk. The round sori that occur on the upper third of the fertile fronds form two rows, and the sori are covered by umbrellalike indusia which are attached to the leaflet by a central stalk.

The roots of *Polystichum* were used by the Cherokee Indians as an ingredient in emetics, as an external application for rheumatism and in a decoction for toothache, chills and stomach aches or bowel complaints.

Polystichum is found on shaded, rocky slopes and in woods and swamp edges. It grows in rather barren soils and tends to cover the surface with mats of old fronds. It is a deterrent to soil erosion and is valued as a garden plant when grown in the shade or in a small amount of sun.

Christmas fern also makes an excellent potted plant. However, as in the wild, old fronds will wither, turn brown and fall off as the plant makes room for new leaves.

Pteris multifida Poiret
Huguenot fern; Spider brake fern
Family: Pteridaceae
(North Carolina, South Carolina, Georgia)

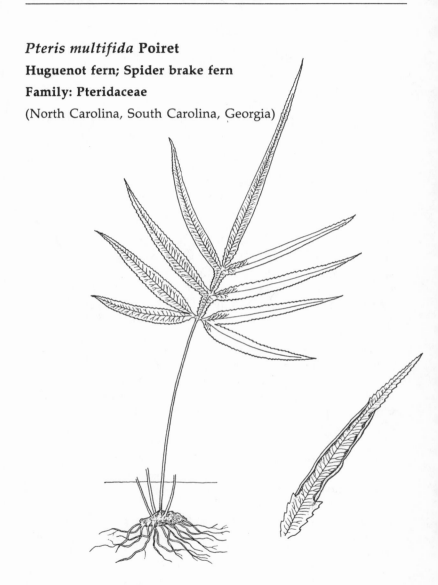

33. *Pteris multifida*/Huguenot fern

The architectural styling of many of the Coastal Plain's old church and graveyards usually includes a masonry wall around the periphery. Often built about 3 feet high and topped by beautifully designed ironworks, these enclosures are as much a part of the church as the steeple. Many masons took advantage of the abundant limestone found here and added this rock, formed from the shells of ancient ocean animals, to the sand mixture to build the walls bordering the church property.

While limestone structures last a long time (the Egyptians used a brownish limestone to build their pyramids), rain and long periods of high humidity over time will cause the limestone to crumble. When it does, pockets of cool, damp, shaded recesses will form and when combined with the high calcium content of the walls, become a suitable habitat for the brake ferns. These ferns will often cascade down the sides of old brick masonry walls like long, green reaching fingers.

One of these brake ferns, *Pteris multifida*, gets the common name of Huguenot fern from its first discovery in a Huguenot cemetery in Charleston, South Carolina, in 1868. Though it is a native plant of Asia, this same species can be found today within the cracks of the walls surrounding many of Charleston's oldest graveyards and churches.

Huguenot fern grows in clusters from a slender rhizome covered by dark brown scales. The immature fronds tend to appear palmate (like a hand) with three unlobed leaflets. Upon maturity, the blades become egg-shaped, 3 to 13 inches long and 8 inches wide. Leaflets are opposite on the rachis, and the 4 to 7 pairs per blade are widely spaced apart. A leafy, wing-type structure is found along the rachis and characterizes this species.

While the sterile frond is wide with serrated or toothed margins, the fertile frond is narrow and entire. The sori are found in a long row along the leaf margins and are not covered by true indusia. Instead, the brake ferns cover their sori with the rolled edges of the leaflet forming a false indusium.

Huguenot fern can be found in masonry and brickworks, rocky woods and sloping hillsides. Fronds appear in April and last until the first frost. The fern grows readily in Coastal Plain gardens and is a pretty addition to a rock garden. It can spread easily by spores and does well in soils to which calcium has been added. The fern is also prized for its adaptability and makes a lovely potted plant.

Pteris vittata Linnaeus
Ladder brake
Family: Pteridaceae
(North Carolina, South Carolina, Georgia)

34. *Pteris vittata*/Ladder brake

The generic name of *Pteris* was given to the brakes by Linnaeus in 1753 from the Greek word *pteris* meaning "wing," and alludes to the shape of the leaflets. Besides Huguenot fern, another species of brake can be found in the Coastal Plain, *Pteris vittata* or ladder brake.

Ladder brake gets its common name from the ladder or steplike appearance of equally spaced, almost opposite leaflets. This fern is a native plant of China and has escaped from cultivation. As a matter of fact, the rhizome of this plant is eaten as a kind of arrowroot in Asia, and the young shoots are also eaten as a vegetable.

The rhizome of the ladder brake is stout, knobby and highly covered with orangish scales. The blades grow 4 to 24 inches long and 5 to 10 inches wide. The stipe and rachis are covered with softly fine scales that can also be found on the veins beneath. Leaflets are simple and linear in shape with toothed margins. As found on its cousin, *Pteris multifida*, the sori are formed in a long row along the margins of the fertile frond and are covered with the reflexed leaf edges to form false indusia.

Ladder brake invades old masonry and waste ground and has been found in rocky woodlands and pinelands. It's a fast-growing, mild-climate plant that can tolerate some sun and can withstand slightly dry conditions. *Pteris vittata* grows particularly well in soils to which limestone has been added.

Woodwardia areolata (Linnaeus) Moore
Netted chain fern
Family: Blechnaceae
(Virginia, North Carolina, South Carolina, Georgia)

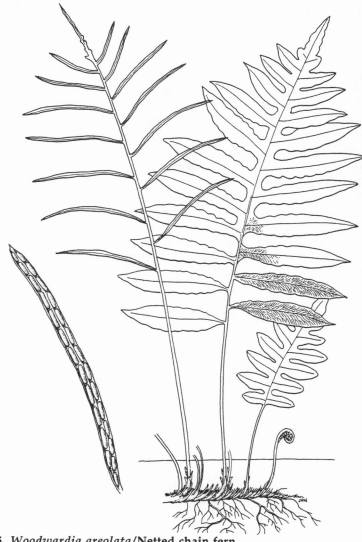

35. *Woodwardia areolata*/Netted chain fern

The most common meaning of the word "chain" means to link, fasten or connect together. The chain ferns, *Woodwardia* species, commemorate the English botanist Thomas J. Woodward (1745–1820), but get their common name from the chainlike rows of sori on the fertile fronds. Botanists organize plants into families by the arrangement of their reproductive structures, and all chain ferns produce the same type of sori. The two chain ferns found in the Coastal Plain, *Woodwardia areolata* and *Woodwardia virginica*, though strikingly dissimilar in sterile blade formation, are therefore linked together in this genus by the similar arrangement of their sori.

The rhizome of *Woodwardia areolata* is moderately covered with light brown scales, and the sterile blade of this fern resembles that of the sensitive fern. The leaflets of the netted chain fern are alternate on the rachis, however, while the leaflets of the sensitive fern are opposite. The 5- to 14-inch sterile blade is deeply cut, and the leaflets produce a wavy, finely toothed margin. A strip of leafy tissue runs along the rachis and gives the blade a thickish appearance. Veins on the sterile frond are often raised, prominent and netted, and hence the species name of "netted" or *areolata*.

Unlike its cousin, Virginia chain fern, the fertile fronds of netted chain fern grow separately and look quite unlike the sterile blade. The stipes of the fertile fronds are usually purple-brown and shiny and are taller than those of the sterile fronds. The chainlike rows of sori appear in the fall along the midrib of the thin, fertile leaflets. These sori are covered by narrow indusia which open toward the midrib and turn deep brown as they mature. Though the sterile fronds die back in the winter, the fertile fronds often remain until spring. Coming across these different-looking "leaves" often presents a puzzle to those unfamiliar with fern identification. The giveaway, however, are those dark, linear sori lining the underside of the blade that are sometimes mistaken for plant disease or decay.

The netted chain fern was used by the North American Indians in basketry and weaving. The fronds would be gathered and the stipe cracked to remove the leathery strands inside. Botanically, these are the vascular strands which are responsible for distributing food, water and minerals throughout the plant.

The chain-fern borer moth, *Papaipema stenocelis*, uses this fern to house its maturing larvae, which emerge from the fern in late summer to fall. This is a small moth with a ½- to 1½-inch wingspan, and front wings of light capucine yellow (yellow orange) fading to a light auburn (lightly tinted, dusty brown, somewhat purplish) with two elongated dots that almost form a vertical line. The hind wings are light to dark capucine buff (light to dark tan), and the hind wing veins are outlined in argus brown.† The larvae bore into the rhizomes of this fern to obtain food.

Netted chain fern grows best in acidic soil and shade and can be found in swamps, bogs and wet pinelands. It is most commonly found in moist ditches along our roadsides. The fern can be easily transplanted to a home garden and grows well in damp acid-humus soil, though it can occasionally become aggressive and take over the garden plot.

36. *Papaipema stenocelis*/**Chain fern borer moth**

---

† Colors are keyed to Robert Ridgway. *Color Standards and Color Nomenclature.* Colors in parentheses are descriptive.

Almost Twice-Cut to Twice-Cut Ferns

37. Twice-cut

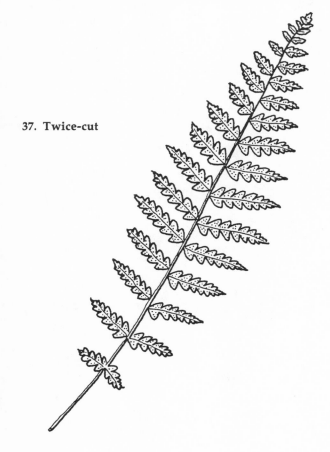

Athyrium asplenioides (Michaux) A. A. Eaton
Also known as: **Athyrium filix-femina (Linnaeus) Roth subsp.** *asplenioides* **(Michaux) Hultén**

Southern lady fern

Family: Woodsiaceae (Aspidiaceae)

(Virginia, North Carolina, South Carolina, Georgia)

38. *Athyrium asplenioides*/**Southern lady fern**

Standing prominently among the other moisture-loving vegetation found along stream banks, the Southern lady fern's size belies its delicate appearance. Though a rather large, clustered fern—2 to 4 feet tall—the plant's light green color and tiny, 1 inch, finely toothed leaflets create an illusion of a much daintier fern.

Southern lady fern grows from a scaly, creeping rhizome that is usually covered with old stipe bases. Stipes are light green, turning reddish toward the base, and a few scales are often present on the lower portion. The frond is egg-shaped and broadest near its base. Leaflets are alternate on the rachis, and subleaflets also are alternate with finely toothed margins. Fertile fronds are generally taller than the sterile and produce numerous, crescent-shaped or oblong indusia-covered sori.

The fern gets its generic name, *Athyrium*, from the Greek word meaning without a door, and refers to the indusia that must dry and wither before releasing the spores. The specific epithet, *asplenioides*, means "like an asplenium" and refers to the linear-shaped indusia.

Southern lady fern grows in swampy woods and thickets, and can be cultivated in a shady to partially sunny garden, in moist, slightly acid soil and tends to spread rapidly.

Dryopteris ludoviciana (Kunze) Small

Southern wood fern; Southern shield fern; Florida wood fern

Family: Dryopteridaceae (Aspidiaceae)

(North Carolina, South Carolina, Georgia)

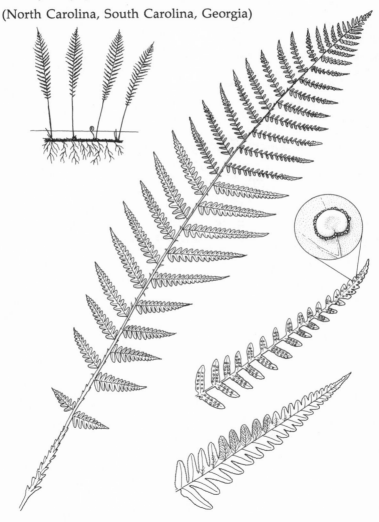

39. *Dryopteris ludoviciana*/Southern wood fern

The term *Dryopteris* was first used by Linnaeus as a specific epithet for the Southern wood fern and probably referred to the habitat of the plant—moist woodlands. But today, the word has been formally given to the wood or shield fern family.

Wood ferns are medium- to large-sized plants, somewhat sturdy in their appearance with stout, creeping, scaly rhizomes, and *Dryopteris ludoviciana* is one wood fern that grows fairly abundantly in the Coastal Plain.

Fronds of the Southern wood fern grow in a short row, are 2 to 4 feet tall and shaped like a narrow oval. The stipe is densely covered with tan-colored scales that help distinguish this species from many look-alikes such as cinnamon and Virginia chain fern. Leaves are evergreen, dark, shiny and somewhat leathery, and the leaflets are alternate with sharply pointed subleaflets.

Round sori appear on the upper portion of the narrower fertile fronds, and the sori are covered with kidney-shaped indusia. As sporangia mature, the leaflets of the fertile frond contract making them appear even slimmer.

The specific epithet, *ludoviciana*, refers to Louisiana, the state where the fern was first discovered by the German botanist, Ludwig. Legend tells us that shortly after Ludwig discovered the fern, he was bitten by a snake and died.

The Cherokee Indians used all species of *Dryopteris* as a decoction to induce vomiting (in preparation for many of their purification and healing ceremonies), as a mouth rinse to relieve toothache and as an external application for rheumatism. In addition, *Dryopteris* ferns found in the West Indies were used for colds and as a general panacea.

The word *Dryopteris* can also mean "of the oak," and because of the plethora of mythology and legends associated with oaks, this word-association surrounds the wood ferns with an air of "mystique."

Southern wood fern is found in swamps, particularly cypress swamps, moist woods, limestone outcrops and stream banks. This is a hardy species and can be grown in woodland gardens.

Dryopteris cristata (Linnaeus) A. Gray
Crested wood fern; Crested shield fern; Narrow swamp fern
Family: Dryopteridaceae (Aspidiaceae)

(Virginia)

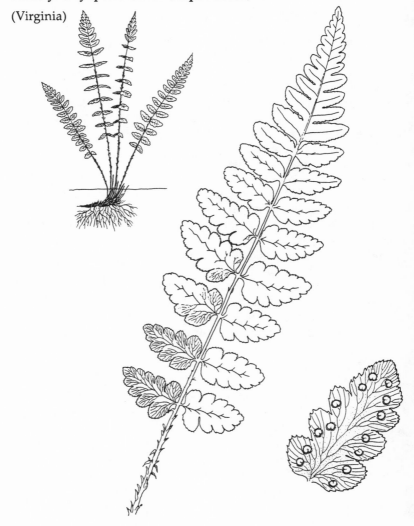

40. *Dryopteris cristata*/Crested wood fern

Another contender for moist areas in woods and swamps is the crested wood fern, *Dryopteris cristata.* This is a lanky-looking fern, for the stipe is somewhat long and the blade which tops it very narrow with widely spaced leaflets. The fern can grow to almost 30 inches tall, while the width of the blade is often less than 6 inches for the sterile and an inch or two narrower for the fertile fronds. In addition, one of the fern's characteristics adds even more to this distinctive appearance. Most of the leaflets on fertile fronds face horizontal on the rachis; that is, they twist in such a way as to lie flat with the plane of the leaflet parallel to the ground, similar in appearance to a thin ladder or venetian blind.

Crested wood fern is evergreen, somewhat bluish green in color, and grows from a stout rhizome that is covered with light brown scales. The stipe is also covered with light brown scales, and the leaflets are mostly opposite on the rachis with those leaflets nearest the base of the frond distinctly triangular in shape. However, as the leaflets ascend the rachis toward the apex, they become reduced in size and the triangular shape disappears. Subleaflets are toothed with pointed tips. Fertile fronds are taller than the sterile and have round sori covered by kidney-shaped indusia.

The specific epithet, *cristata,* means "crest," though the reason Linnaeus gave this fern such a reference has not been discovered. In English heraldry, ferns were often used as emblems for a particular family's helmet or as the heraldic device placed above the shield in a coat of arms. Although sheer speculation, perhaps the idea of this fern used as a plume to decorate a helmet inspired Linnaeus.

Medicinally, crested wood fern has been used in the United States to relieve chest phlegm, to expel worms and to help break fevers.

Dryopteris cristata can be found in moist woods, swamps and marshes and can be cultivated in shady, moderately acid soil.

Dryopteris celsa (W. Palmer) Small
Log fern
Family: Dryopteridaceae (Aspidiaceae)
(Virginia, North Carolina)

41. *Dryopteris celsa*/**Log fern**

Another of the wood ferns, *Dryopteris celsa*, is a rather large evergreen plant. Light to dark brown scales cover the creeping rhizome, and the light green stipe is also covered with brown scales. Fronds grow in short rows that can reach 2 to 4 feet high. The blade is oblong and tapers toward the apex. The leaflets are alternate on the rachis, and subleaflets have sharply pointed margins. Fertile fronds produce round sori that are covered by horseshoe-shaped indusia.

The specific epithet, *celsa*, means "held high" and refers to the plant's habit of growing atop logs and humus. This characteristic habitat also gives the plant its common name of log fern. The sterile blades of this fern and those of Southern wood fern are so similar that telling the two apart may well depend, for the novice at least, on where the plant is found.

Log fern is not overly common, but can be found in swamps, wet woods and seepage ditches where the soil is acidic. The fern was first discovered in Virginia's Great Dismal Swamp, and experts believe this species to be a hybrid between *Dryopteris goldiana* and *Dryopteris ludoviciana*. The plant is not cultivated.

Osmunda cinnamomea Linnaeus
Cinnamon fern
Family: Osmundaceae

(Virginia, North Carolina, South Carolina, Georgia)

42. *Osmunda cinnamomea*/**Cinnamon fern**

For most of the Coastal Plain the arrival of the fall season is subtle. Vibrant greens of summer almost imperceptibly fade into a yellow-green, dull brown color that can be easily missed when viewing the same landscape each day. A trip away from the Coastal Plain and a return home is usually necessary before the change is even realized. Though our falls are not usually as picturesque as those in colder climates, we, nonetheless, have some hardwood habitats that give us our share, if only in small quantities, of the reds, oranges, golds and crimsons we usually associate with this season. One plant which gives us a portion of our fall color is the cinnamon fern, for during this season the tall, graceful fronds become a beautiful cinnamon brown color.

Cinnamon fern grows from a stout, scaleless, woody rhizome that usually becomes covered with old roots and stipe bases and on old plants may arise from the ground like the trunk of a tree fern. Black, wiry roots grow from the rhizome and are often densely matted together.

The spring fiddleheads are covered with silvery, white hairs that later turn to a cinnamon color as the fern uncoils. The sterile blades are arranged in a symmetrical crown reaching heights of 2 to 5 feet. Stipes are light-colored and covered with tufts of red-brown colored "wool" which when crushed smells like cinnamon and is one possible source for this fern's common name. Blades are broadly lance-shaped with leaflets alternate or nearly opposite on the rachis. Each leaflet is cut into oblong divisions that almost reach the midvein.

The fertile fronds differ in appearance from the sterile blades, and grow in the spring from the center of the crown—first light green in color and then turning a rich cinnamon color upon maturity. Fertile fronds are narrower, erect and about the same height as the sterile leaves with clustered, reddish-brown, round sori without indusia. After the spores have been dispersed, the fertile frond withers, but the tufts of wooly, brown hairs remain on the stipes and make identification of the sterile fronds easy.

Like the sensitive fern, *Osmunda cinnamomea* occasionally produces blades that appear to be a cross between the sterile and fertile fronds. Some taxonomists have named this form, variety *frondosa*. This variety was collected from Myrtle Beach, South

Carolina, in the fall of 1980 from a road construction site and again in the spring of 1981 after Hurricane David had swept through that area in 1979. However, most taxonomists attribute this abnormality to environmental factors and simply keep the fern as the species *Osmunda cinnamomea*.

The osmunda borer moth, *Papaipema speciosissima*, deposits its larvae on the roots, stipes or rhizomes of the cinnamon fern. This moth is similar to the species that attacks the chain fern, except the osmunda borer is larger with a 1¾ to 2 inch wingspan. Its front wings are bright capucine yellow (bright orange) blending into an antique brown on the edges with its median line bending sharply—almost like an angle bracket. Spots on the front wings are white or brown, and the hind wings are light to dark capucine buff (dusty orangish brown) fading to a dusty auburn on the edges. Veins are outlined in argus brown (milk chocolate brown).* The moth is often spotted in association with *Osmunda* in September and October.

The sterile fronds of the cinnamon fern die back each winter, but the rhizome sends up new fiddleheads in the spring. The tightly coiled, woolly covered croziers can be eaten before they unfurl and after the hairs have been rubbed off with the fingers. In fact, folklore says that if you take a bite from the first cinnamon fern of the season, you can be assured of a toothache-

43. *Papaipema speciosissima/* **Osmunda borer moth**

free year. These crisp vegetables can be eaten raw and prepared like green beans, and the Cherokee Indians used them as a spring tonic. The Menomini Indians would make a soup from the young fronds by boiling them in water. Along the base of the plant, attached to the rhizome, are the buds of future fronds. These buds

---

* Colors are keyed to Robert Ridgway. *Color Standards and Color Nomenclature.* Colors in parentheses are descriptive.

have been called "bag onions," and can be gathered and eaten like raw cabbage. The heart of the unrolled crown, too, is crisp and tender and eaten as asparagus.

The Cherokees also used the cinnamon fern for snake bites and as a "chew root." A portion of the root or rhizome would be chewed, some swallowed and the rest applied to a wound. Roots were also used as a decoction for chills and as an aid for rheumatism. Cinnamon fern rhizomes have also been used for rooting and growing orchids, though harvesting this part of the fern destroys the plant. In Japan the fine hairs of the young fronds are mixed with wool and made into raincoats.

The meaning of the word *Osmunda* has several different interpretations. The word *osmunda* is said to mean "flowering fern," not because the plant actually produces flowers, but when the fertile fronds are ripe with mature sori, their growth pattern and clustered appearance resemble tiny, red-brown "blossoms." *Osmund* is also a Saxon word meaning domestic peace from the words *os* (house) and *mund* (peace). In addition, some authorities believe that Linnaeus named the plant *Osmunda* in 1753 not for any particular meaning of the word but to honor Osmunder, the Saxon god.† We may never know which definition is the actual reason for the fern's name, but by considering the ideas implied by these interpretations, we can gain a sense of the plant's lore, legend and mystery.

Osmunda cinnamomea thrives in the acidic soil of moist and shady places, such as marshes, swamps, ditches and stream banks. Along sunny edges of woodlots, these large, early spring ferns and "flowering" fronds are breathtaking against the newly leafing trees and shrubs and are a sure sign that summer is not far behind. Cinnamon fern is easily transplanted to the home garden and grows best in moist, shady soil to which fine loam has been added.

---

† Frances Theodora Parsons, *How to Know the Ferns: A Guide to the Names, Haunts and Habits of our Common Ferns* (New York: Dover Publications, 1962) 62-63. Also: M. Grieve, *A Modern Herbal: The Medicinal, Culinary, Cosmetic and Economic Properties, Cultivation and Fork-lore of Herbs, Grasses, Fungi, Shrubs & Trees with Their Modern Scientific Uses—In Two Volumes* (New York: Dover Publications, 1982) 308. Lloyd H. Snyder, Jr. and James G. Bruce, *Field Guide to the Ferns and Other Pteridophytes of Georgia* (Athens: University of Georgia Press, 1986) 34.

Osmunda claytonia **Linnaeus**
Interrupted fern
Family: Osmundaceae
(Virginia)

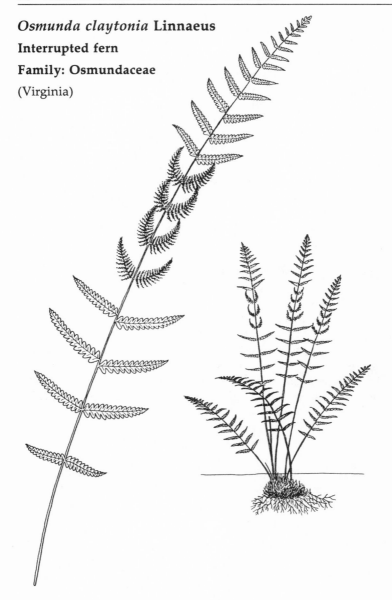

44. *Osmunda claytoniana*/Interrupted fern

Growing robustly in crowns, the interrupted fern is often mistaken for its cousin, cinnamon fern. Both grow in clusters, both are rather tall (2 to 4 feet) and both have large, stout rhizomes and black, wiry roots and light-colored stipes. Yet during the early spring when the sori appear and ripen, there is no confusing these two ferns.

When fruiting, the fertile frond of the interrupted fern is just as its common name implies—disrupted. The beautiful symmetry of its green leaves is *interrupted* by smaller, constricted leaflets lined with dark brown, spherical sporangia. These fertile sporangia grow from the central portion of the rachis, with sterile leaflets below and above it. In contrast, cinnamon fern produces entirely separate sterile and fertile fronds.

Other subtle differences exist. After ripening, the fertile leaflets wither and drop from the interrupted fern, leaving a large space on the stipe. In this fern, too, the subleaflets of the sterile fronds overlap, while those in cinnamon fern do not. In addition, the leaflets below the fertile leaflet portion of the rachis are widely spaced apart compared to the sterile fronds of the same plant. Interrupted fern does not have the little tufts of brown "wool" in the leaf axils as does the cinnamon fern. And the interrupted fern occupies a somewhat dryer, stonier habitat than the cinnamon fern, which prefers a moister environment.

Interrupted fern gets its specific epithet in honor of Virginia botanist, John Clayton. It is found in a few scattered locations in Virginia's Coastal Plain but is more widespread in the mountain region. *Osmunda claytonia* can also be found in the foothill and mountain regions of North Carolina, South Carolina and Georgia. While interrupted fern is most often found in dryer locations than cinnamon fern, it will grow in rich woodlands and slopes. It can be cultivated in moist, circumneutral soil in partial or full shade.

Osmunda regalis var. spectabilis (Willdenow) A. Gray
Royal fern
Family: Osmundaceae

(Virginia, North Carolina, South Carolina, Georgia)

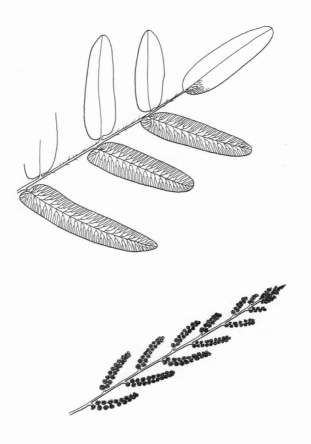

45. *Osmunda regalis* **var.** *spectabilis/***Royal fern**

The pale translucent green of the royal fern growing along marsh edges and glistening in the sunlight turns one's imagination to primordial forests, for the shape of this fern can easily be mistaken for a tree fern or an immature locust tree.

This is a regal plant: tall and graceful and one of our largest ferns. As in the fern *Osmunda cinnamomea*, the rhizome is stout and scaleless. The rhizome of this species can rise above the ground with old stipe-bases to form a short "trunk." This structure gives the fern its treelike appearance. Royal fern forms a graceful cluster of fronds that can grow from 19 to 60 inches long. Sterile blades are egg-shaped and have round-tipped, alternate leaflets. When the fern grows in the shade, the leaflets turn a bright green against the reddish stalks. In full sunlight, the leaflets are a pale, almost translucent green.

Fertile leaflets are terminal on the lower, sterile portions of some fronds. Sori are globular without indusia and appear in mid-summer.

The osmunda borer moth, *Papaipema speciosissima*, not only deposits its larvae on the cinnamon fern, but does so on this species as well.

The rhizomes are used to grow orchids and are often called Osmund fibers. The white, fleshy inner part of the rhizome is edible but has a rather pungent taste. In addition, the royal fern is also noted for its medicinal value, and one source says the word *Osmund* means "to cleanse," in reference to its medicinal proper-ties.‡ A decoction from the rhizome was used for clearing internal obstructions, soothing coughs and for jaundice, if taken early. The mucilage (gummy or gelatinous sap) was used in treating coughs and diarrhea and made a good ointment for sprains, bruises and wounds. When mixed with brandy, the mucilage was once a popular rub for backaches. A conserve from the roots was used for rickets. Boiled into an ointment, roots were used for treating broken bones and to ease the colic and diseases of the spleen.

A fiber from the royal fern is obtained from the rhizome, but soaking or beating is often necessary before the fibers can be

---

‡ Grieve, *A Modern Herbal*, 308.

extracted. After drying, they can be worked into such things as rope, twine, cloth, netting, mats or baskets.

In his sixteenth-century *Herbal,* John Gerard tells us that *Osmunda regalis* was called Osmund the Waterman, alluding to the fern's preference for wet marshes. A certain Osmund, says one legend, was living at Loch Tyne (Scotland) when the Danes began an attack. The resourceful Osmund hid his wife and child on an island of flowering ferns, thus saving them. When the child grew up, she then named these plants after her father.

Another story describes the metallurgy of early medieval Europe when iron was made directly from the bog iron ore found on pond bottoms and in swampy areas. The pieces of ore and the rough masses of iron were called osmunds. Since the royal fern grew in the same location as the bog iron, the association could account for the name.

In some parts of Europe, the royal fern is dedicated to St. Christopher, the saint who waded across the river with the Christ-child on his shoulders. Because of the fern's affinity for water, the association between the saint and the fern is made. In addition, the festival of St. Christopher falls on July 25. Some folklorists believe that since the royal fern reaches maturity by St. Christopher's Day, it is given the name "water fern" or Osmunda.

Like *Osmunda cinnamomea,* the royal fern dies back each winter, but the persistent rhizomes send out smooth, wine-colored croziers each spring to unfurl into one of the Coastal Plain's most exquisite ferns. *Osmunda regalis* can be found in marshes, swamps, stream valleys and wet woods. It is easily transplanted, thrives in moist, acid soil and tolerates some shade.

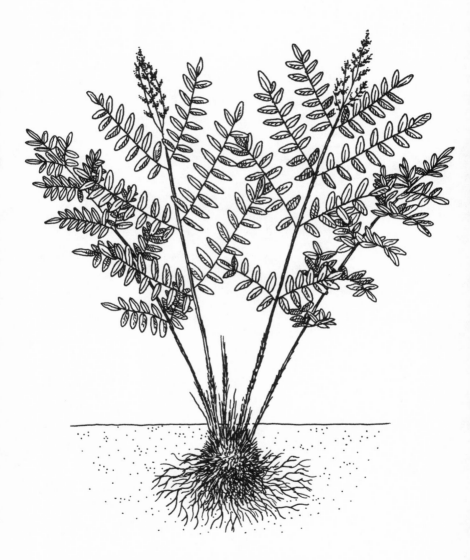

Osmunda regalis var. *spectabilis* growth pattern

Thelypteris palustris Schott
Also known as: Dryopteris thelypteris **(Linnaeus) A. Gray**

Marsh fern

Family: Thelypteridaceae (Aspidiaceae)

(Virginia, North Carolina, South Carolina, Georgia)

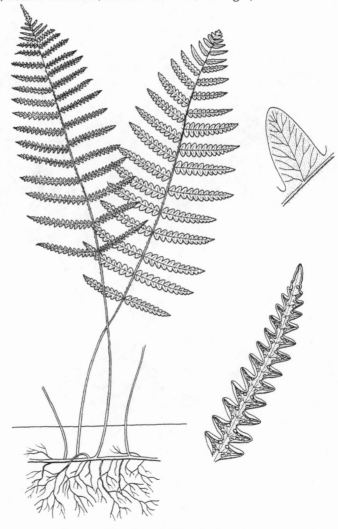

46. *Thelypteris palustris*/**Marsh fern**

A botanical definition for a marsh is a region of vegetation where the water table is at or just below the soil level. Although one often thinks of saltwater marshes when speaking of the marsh, the Coastal Plain is also filled with freshwater marshes—expanses of wetlands most often found near rivers and upstream from salt marshes. Predominant plant species include sweetflag (*Acorus calamus*), alligatorweed (*Alternanthera philoxeroides*), burmarigold (*Bidens* species), sedges (*Carex* species), arrow-arum (*Peltandra virginica*), pickerelweed (*Pontederia cordata*), swamp rose (*Rosa palustris*), cattails (*Typha* species), wild rice (*Zizania aquatica*) and giant cutgrass (*Zizaniopsis mileacea*). In addition to numerous other rushes, sedges and grasses, the delicate-looking marsh fern can be found.

Thelypteris palustris begins its above-ground life as most other ferns—curled like a crozier. Yet while other fiddleheads are sideways flattened, the marsh fern fiddlehead is round like a small ball. It is a large, coarse, rather stiff, non-evergreen fern, 15 to 36 inches tall. The stipe is long, often longer than the oval-shaped blade, with tiny scales at the base but smooth above. Leaflets are barely opposite, and subleaflets are oblong and cut almost to the midrib. A close look at these leaflets will show that the veins are forked at the ends. In addition, the lowest pair of leaflets are often a bit shorter than those of the upper part of the fern and are perpendicular to the stipe. These characteristics—the forked veins and the vertical leaflets—are different in other *Thelypteris* species and helps to tell them apart.

Fertile fronds are similar to the sterile, but are often taller. The round sori are found near the leaflet margins and are covered with small, kidney-shaped indusia. As the sori mature and turn brown, the leaflets of the fertile frond curl over the sori, and the leaflets lose the rounded shape of their apex and appear pointed and much thinner than the sterile leaves.

The fern's generic name alludes to its appearance and habitat. *Thelypteris* means female and tender and refers to the fern's delicate appearance. *Palustris*, on the other hand, means "of the marsh" and refers to the plant's habitat.

Marsh fern can also be found from spring through fall in wet, swampy woods, thickets and the edges of swamps. Marsh fern has an aggressive tendency and tends to take over a garden.

Thelypteris kunthii (Desvaux) Morton
Also known as: ***Thelypteris normalis* (Carl Christensen) Moxley**

Widespread maiden fern

Family: Thelypteridaceae (Aspidiaceae)

(North Carolina, South Carolina, Georgia)

47. *Thelypteris kunthii*/Widespread maiden fern

Widespread maiden fern is another moisture-loving plant and prefers soils that are fairly alkaline.

It's a large, sturdy plant, from 21 to almost 48 inches tall, with narrowly triangular fronds growing next to one another in short rows. The stipe is light-colored and topped by a lance-shaped blade. Leaflets are almost opposite, with long, tapering subleaflets cut almost three-quarters to the midrib. Veins are slightly hairy above and beneath and are usually not forked. (These last two characteristics—leaflets cut three-quarters to the midrib and non-forked veins—help to distinguish *Thelypteris kunthii* from *Thelypteris palustris*.) The last leaflets of the blade are about the same size or slightly longer than the leaflets above them.

Fertile fronds bear kidney-shaped indusia that grow between the margin and midvein of the leaflet, and the round sori mature from late spring to summer.

Thelypteris kunthii has been used in the West Indies on wounds. The plant was parched and beaten and then sprinkled on the affected area. Another preparation boiled the fern; the decoction was used to clean and help close open cuts. The Mexican Kickapoo Indians made a decoction of the fern for bathing an aching ear. When combined with maidenhair fern, the decoction was consumed before breakfast for four consecutive days as a contraceptive after intercourse. In addition, a decoction blending this fern, maidenhair fern and camphor plant (*Heterotheca latifolia*) was drunk by women to stop excessive bleeding either from the menstrual cycle, miscarriage or abortion.

Thelypteris kunthii can be found in moist, calcareous soils, rock crevices, swampy woods and drainage ditches.

Thelypteris hexagonoptera (Michaux) Weatherby

Broad beech fern

Family: Thelypteridaceae (Aspidiaceae)

(North Carolina, South Carolina, Georgia)

48. *Thelypteris hexagonoptera*/Broad beech fern

Summer heat comes early to the Coastal Plain, and by mid-May many folks seek the cooling relief offered by its beaches and ocean waters. Yet sprinkled throughout the Coastal Plain's diverse landscape are pockets of rich forests which offer their own kind of refuge.

These are the beech forests, also called river bluffs or beech ravines. Here, cathedral beech trees, *Fagus grandifolia*, provide a canopy over the dogwoods, sassafras, holly, redbud and musclewood trees (*Carpinus caroliniana*) also found in this lush area. Stream waters branch off from the nearby river to create a netted pattern through the forest's slopes and glens, while filtered sunlight dapples the rich, moist soil and the smaller plants—heartleaf, ginger, crane-fly orchid and ladies tresses—growing there. Ferns, too, enjoy this rich company, and on a walk through the refreshing shade and quiet, one is likely to find the Christmas fern, rattlesnake fern and the fern named after this habitat: the broad beech fern.

The scaly, creeping rhizome of the broad beech fern sends up new fronds in rows, and the fronds often appear scattered. Though somewhat tall—from 13 to just over 24 inches—the fern appears delicate against the backdrop of the smooth-gray bark of the tall beech trees. The thin stipe is light-colored, somewhat brittle and is topped by the green, slightly hairy blade. The blade is widest at its base, giving the fern its distinctive triangular shape. Leaflets are opposite, cut almost to the midvein and lobed or toothed. Along the rachis (the central axis found within the blade portion of the fern) is a conspicuous wing—an extension of the green, leafy tissue.

Fertile fronds are similar to the sterile and contain small, round sori without indusia, which grow near the margins of the leaflets.

Thelypteris hexagonoptera grows well in woodlands, thickets and ravines in moist, rich soil. When the summer heat becomes unbearable or when the busyness of the day sends one seeking respite, the beech forests are a wonderfully serene escape, and the broad beech fern found there, an understanding, undemanding companion.

Thelypteris hexagonoptera can be cultivated and tends to spread rapidly. It dies back in winter and when it receives too much sun.

Thelypteris noveboracensis **(Linnaeus) Nieuwland**
New York fern
Family: Thelypteridaceae (Aspidiaceae)
(Virginia, North Carolina)

49. *Thelypteris noveboracensis*/**New York fern**

Bright lights, Madison Avenue, Broadway plays, fast-pace, loud noises, terrifying traffic and New York fern? Some authorities believe this fern was named by Linnaeus because he was sent the fern from that region. Other accounts believe the fern was sent to him from Canada. Either way, in today's associations with that city, New York fern may seem quite inappropriately named. However, outside bustling New York City, the region is richly filled with beautiful hardwood forests, a habitat also found in Virginia and North Carolina and where one is likely to find this fern growing.

Fronds are 11 to almost 24 inches tall with leaflets opposite or alternate on the rachis. Compared to the other *Thelypteris*, New York fern is quite distinct with its diamond-shaped blade and tapering, silvery-haired leaflets—each pair getting smaller as they descend the rachis until it seems only a bit of green tissue is left. Subleaflets are deeply cut almost to the midvein.

Fertile fronds contain kidney-shaped, sparsely hairy indusia and round sori, which are found near the leaflet margins and mature from late spring through the summer.

Thelypteris noveboracensis grows in moist thickets, woodlands and swamps and seems to grow best in subacidic to acidic soil. The fern can be easily cultivated but will die back in winter.

Thelypteris dentata (Forsskal) E. P. St. John
Downy maiden fern
Family: Thelypteridaceae (Aspidiaceae)
(South Carolina, Georgia)

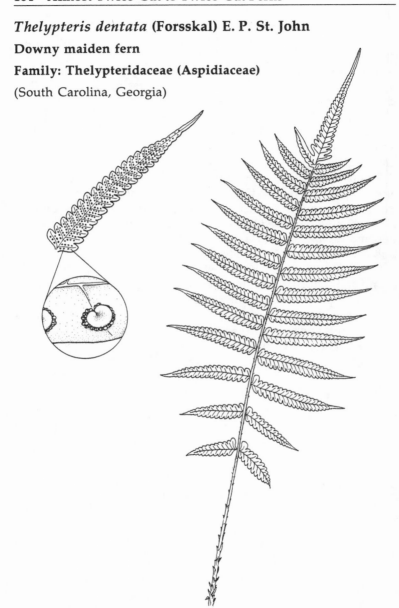

50. *Thelypteris dentata*/Downy maiden fern

Living up to its common name, the downy maiden fern is covered by tiny hairs or trichomes. Because of these short trichomes, the purplish stipe, as well as the leaflets, feels rough to the touch.

Downy maiden fern is a medium to large fern growing from 15 inches to just over 36 inches tall. Its rhizome is creeping and scaly, and fronds are produced in clusters.

The blade is widest in the middle and lance-shaped. As in many of the other *Thelypteris* species, leaflets are either alternate or opposite on the rachis. The lowest pair of leaflets are shorter than those above and point downward. Leaflets are cut two-thirds to the midvein forming oval subleaflets. A close look at the subleaflets will show the vein nearest the midvein connected from one leaflet to another. Fertile fronds have kidney-shaped indusia covering small, round sori.

Downy maiden fern grows in damp woods, limestone sinks and along streams or rivers.

Woodsia obtusa (Sprengel) Torrey

Blunt-lobed woodsia

Family: Woodsiaceae (Aspidiaceae)

(Virginia, North Carolina, South Carolina, Georgia)

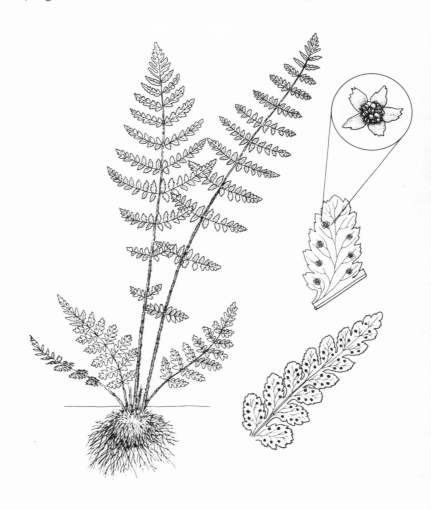

51. *Woodsia obtusa*/Blunt-lobed woodsia

Woodsia obtusa is a small, frilly-leaved fern that grows 8 to 20 inches high from a scaly, creeping rhizome. Light green, diamond-shaped blades top a light-colored, scaly stipe. Leaflets are almost opposite on the rachis, and subleaflets are bluntly lobed. The fertile fronds produce unusual sori. Round sporangia are clustered within the cuplike indusia. Upon maturity the indusia split into ribbonlike filaments forming tiny star-shaped structures. The indusia are secured to the leaflet with the clustered sporangia on top of them and are reminiscent of the "flowers" created from the bottom halves of pine cones.

Clusters of woodsia are often found in shaded woodlands, the kind of habitat often associated with the Greek woodland god, Pan. Pan is often depicted as half-goat and half-man with pointed ears and goat horns; he reigned over fertility and protected herds and shepherds. His powers later increased to include healing and prophesying; he created the panpipes and became the leader of the woodland spirits. Though Pan is considered a "lusty" god, he is said to have enjoyed quiet, lonely places. Legend tells us that there, midst ancient trees and rippling stream waters, Pan would often take a nap, but if he were awakened, his terrible anger would rage. The term "panic" is said to come from Pan's terrifying looks as well as his formidable anger. Therefore, when searching for the blunt-lobed woodsia, step quietly along the wooded paths!

Though this fern is most abundant in our mountain regions, colonies can be found in rocky woods, along stream banks, in limestone, woodlands and sometimes on masonry walls. Blunt-lobed woodsia can be cultivated in a shady location in circum-neutral soil and makes an attractive addition to a rock garden.

Woodwardia virginica (Linnaeus) J. E. Smith
Virginia chain fern
Family: Blechnaceae
(Virginia, North Carolina, South Carolina, Georgia)

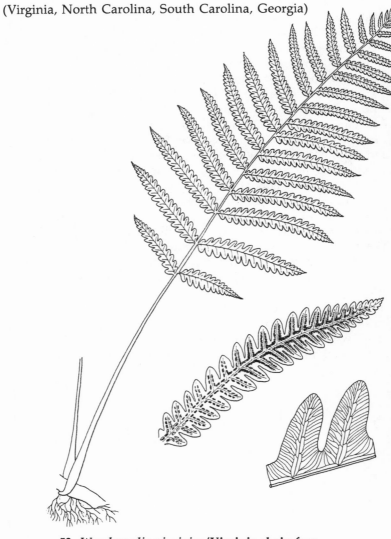

52. *Woodwardia virginica*/**Virginia chain fern**

The Virginia chain fern has two chainlike characteristics: (1) the growth pattern of its rhizome and sterile fronds and (2) the arrangement of its sori on the fertile frond.

Woodwardia virginica grows from a "creeping" rhizome. This means that each year one end of the rhizome dies back while the other end grows new tissue. In this way the plant slowly moves across the forest floor. The stout, scaly, red-brown rhizome of Virginia chain fern, the underground storage system for the plant, sends out new fronds one after the other in long "rows." In addition, like its relative *Woodwardia areolata*, the sori of Virginia chain fern are arranged in chainlike rows on the fertile frond.

The leathery, 12 to 31 inch sterile blade has such deeply cut leaflets that it could almost be considered twice-divided. The frond is broadest in the middle, with leaflets almost opposite and usually close together. *Woodwardia virginica* is often mistaken for the cinnamon fern but lacks the clustered growth pattern and woolly brown hairs found on that species. In addition, the stipe of Virginia chain fern is dark-colored, while that of the cinnamon fern is light green to straw-colored.

The sterile and fertile fronds of Virginia chain fern are similar in appearance, especially when compared with the different looking sterile and fertile fronds of *Woodwardia areolata*. The sori appear during the summer months, and the leathery indusia cover the dark brown sori. Because of the similar coloration, the indusia are almost inconspicuous.

Virginia chain fern was used in basketry much like *Woodwardia areolata*. In addition, North Carolina Indians found the leaves of this species to be astringent and used the plant in applications where constriction was needed.

The chain fern borer moth also uses this species of *Woodwardia* to deposit its eggs. Other insects or moths will use the tips of this fern as their home by rolling the tip over and onto itself where the larvae will remain until they pupate.

Virginia chain fern grows in sunny or shady areas, acid soils, bogs, thickets and wet pinelands, and the fern is often found in standing water. In woodland conditions Virginia chain fern often grows alongside the sweet pepper bush, *Clethra alnifolia*; pitcher plants, *Sarracenia* species; and the pink meadow beauty, *Rhexia virginica.* It dies back in the winter and, unlike *Woodwardia areolata*, does not leave any conspicuous fertile fronds to divulge its hiding place until the new leaves appear in the spring.

This is an aggressive fern and will readily take over a garden. However, it is a perfect plant for water-logged, muddy barrens where little else will grow.

Almost Thrice-Cut, Thrice-Cut or Lacy Ferns

53. Thrice-cut

Adiantum capillus-veneris Linnaeus
Southern maidenhair
Family: Adiantaceae (Pteridaceae)

(North Carolina, South Carolina, Georgia)

54. *Adiantum capillus-veneris*/**Southern maidenhair**

Venus, also known as Aphrodite, is the laughter-loving goddess of love and beauty said to have risen from the sea with her beautifully flowing tresses undampened by the water. Poets paint pictures of this deity surrounded by radiant light, joy, loveliness, laughing seas and masses of flowers:

> The breath of the west wind bore her
> Over the sounding sea,
> Up from the delicate foam,
> To her wave-ringed Cyprus, her isle.
> And the Hours golden-wreathed
> Welcomed her joyously.
> They clad her in raiment immortal.
> And brought her to the gods.
> Wonder seized them all as they saw
> Violet-crowed Cyntherea.*
>
> Homer

The delicate beauty and the water-repellent qualities of the maidenhair fern must have inspired Linnaeus when he named this plant, for the word *Adiantum* means unmoistened, and *capillus-veneris* means "Venus' hair." The tribute paid to Venus by Homer is certainly equal to the one Linnaeus paid to the maidenhair fern when he named it.

As one of the Coastal Plain's most delicate and attractive ferns, Southern maidenhair is a favorite. From its creeping rhizome grow brittle, arching, red-black colored stipes. Fringing these are lacy blades, as long as 20 inches, with very thin, fan-shaped leaflets up to ⅜ inch in length. Sori are shaped like half-moons and are borne on the outer edges of the leaf margins, which curl over the sori to form false indusia. The waxy epidermis of each leaflet gives the fern its water-repellent properties.

Lye soap, made from maidenhair ashes, fat and oil, was used as a medicinal shampoo and as a treatment of skin diseases. John Gerard, a sixteenth-century herbalist, said of maidenhair: "It consumeth and wasteth away the King's Evil and other hard swellings,

---

* Quoted in Edith Hamilton, *Mythology* (New York: Grosset & Dunlap, 1978) 33.

and it maketh the haire of the head or beard to grow that is fallen and pulled off."

But Southern maidenhair was used for more than hair care. Early herbalists also prescribed this plant's medicinal qualities for relieving asthma, stones, disorders of the spleen, snakebite, coughs, chest congestion and as a mildly stimulating tonic.

According to Nicholas Culpepper, a seventeenth-century herbalist, an infusion of the leaves was used to reduce the swelling and congestion of the mucus membranes in the nose and throat. To relieve coughs, one ounce of the leaves would be infused in a pint of boiling water, honey added and then made into a syrup. In fact, Montpellier, France, was the origin of Syrup of Capillaire, a cough medicine made by using fresh maidenhair fronds, orange-flower water and honey. Another recipe for a similar cough syrup called for using dried fronds, orange juice, licorice root, water and sugar.

Southern maidenhair was also used in decoctions for tea (when brewed very strongly it was used as an emetic), extracts and tinctures. The main constituents of the plant include tannic acid, gallic acid and traces of an essential oil which produce a pleasant tonic flavor. Syrups have been used as flavor modifiers, and tinctures have been included in hair tonics and alcoholic beverages.

In North America Southern maidenhair was used as a cure for rickets in children, and the entire plant was steamed for use in smallpox cures. In the eighteenth and nineteenth centuries, the fern often garnished sweet dishes.

The Navajo Indians made an infusion of the fern and used the blend to relieve bee stings and centipede bites. For the Navajo the growth pattern of the Southern maidenhair with its leaves "just touching here and there" suggested that the fern could be used in cases of insanity. The remedy included maidenhair fern and three additional plants, and the patient was made to smoke this mixture.

The leaves of *Adiantum capillus-veneris* are an official drug in Europe, and the plant is used to stimulate the menstrual flow. As the fern is also mildly diuretic, it was employed to treat impurities of the kidneys.

Members of the Southern Sotho tribe of Africa smoke the leaves of this plant to relieve head and chest colds. In Madeira the plant was used as a soothing beverage or a sweet. In Mexico and Argentina Southern maidenhair is given to relieve sore throat and rheumatism, to help expedite the labor of childbirth, and in Mexico used as an aperitif. Fronds are employed for chest diseases in the Philippines, and the plant is used in the Yucatan to dissolve urinary calcifications.

The dark, slender stipes of Southern maidenhair have been split to make strands; these are used to weave black designs and patterns in coiled basketry.

The Coastal Plain is graced by the delicate beauty of this fern, and preserving this plant and its habitat will ensure the enjoyment of *Adiantum* for future generations. Southern maidenhair is found on shady calcareous (calcium or lime-rich) slopes, masonry, moist limestone cliffs and sink walls.

Although the ferns make beautiful houseplants, the habitat and occurrence of *Adiantum* in the Coastal Plain area is not overly common, so please do not gather this plant from the wild. Many professional nurseries can provide species of wild plants for cultivation.

Adiantum pedatum Linnaeus
Northern maidenhair
Family: Adiantaceae (Pteridaceae)

(Virginia, North Carolina, South Carolina, Georgia)

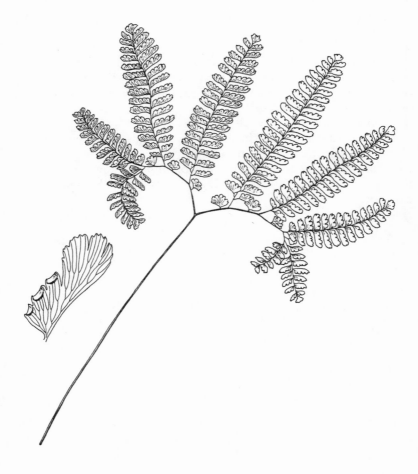

55. *Adiantum pedatum*/Northern maidenhair

Northern maidenhair is strikingly beautiful. The form of its leaves is so different from other ferns that recognition is easy even without looking at the sori.

From thin, shiny, brownish-black stipes comes a forked blade topped with delicate, fan-shaped leaflets. These graceful leaves, unlike many other ferns, grow horizontally from the stipe and appear like a green bridal veil—the curving rachis like the bridal crown and the leaflets like the gossamer netting that covers the bride's face. It is semicircular or horseshoe in shape with leaflets alternate and oblong. The word *pedatum* means feet, and with a good imagination one can see the similarity between the delicate leaflets and its specific epithet. Another authority sees a connection of the word *pedatum* to the outline of the blade—each end tapering like the toes.

Northern maidenhair grows from 18 to just over 24 inches tall. The sori that appear on the underside of the leaflets are covered by true indusia, and like its cousin Southern maidenhair, the leaf margins roll over these sori to form false indusia as well.

Adiantum pedatum has been used in much the same ways as *A. capillus-veneris*. It has been made into cough syrup, used for fevers, colds, asthma and made into a tea and taken as a tonic. The Cherokee Indians used the plant in a tea for rheumatism and would smoke the powdered leaves for heart trouble and asthma. The entire plant was also steeped and blown over the feverish parts of the patient. In addition, the roots were mixed with *Polystichum acrostichoides* (Christmas fern), *Osmunda cinnamomea* (cinnamon fern), blended with water into a decoction and applied to rheumatic muscles.

The Forest Potawatomi Indians (Wisconsin) used an infusion of the root of the northern maidenhair as a tea to cure caked breasts in nursing mothers. The fern was also made into a decoction for hoarseness, flu and pleurisy. In addition, the black stipes were carried as a hunting charm to bring good luck in the hunt. These same shiny black stipes were also used by other American Indians in their basketry.

Typically, *Adiantum pedatum* is considered a Northern species. Though the fern is found most abundantly in Virginia, several scattered collections have been made throughout the Coastal Plain of North Carolina, South Carolina and Georgia. However, the plant can be readily found in the mountains of these three states in rich woods, shady slopes and moist soils. It's a perfect garden fern, though it does die back in winter, and grows best in rich, loose, well-drained humus soil away from direct sunlight. The rhizome and fronds must be kept moist until the plant is firmly established.

Adiantum pedatum **growth pattern**

Botrychium virginianum (Linnaeus) Swartz

Rattlesnake fern; Grapefern; "Indicator" or "Sang sign"

Family: Ophioglossaceae

(Virginia, North Carolina, South Carolina, Georgia)

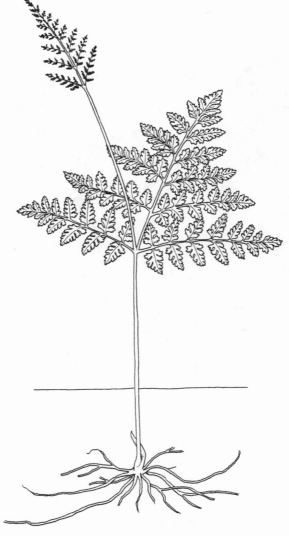

56. *Botrychium virginianum*/Rattlesnake fern

Botrychium virginianum is a lacy-looking fern, yet unlike most ferns that arise from the ground in coiled fiddleheads, the *Botrychiums* develop their leaves underground and when above the soil, they unfold as they expand. The sterile frond is bright green, 3 to 9 inches long, triangular in shape and highly dissected.

The fertile portion of the frond arises from the juncture of the sterile blade in late spring or early summer and often grows 7½ to 15½ inches above the pretty, sterile leaf. The clusters of sporangia that top the fertile frond are bright yellow, spherical and without indusia. Upon maturity, the spore cases split horizontally across the center to expel the cream-colored spores. These sporangia reminded the early observers of rattles found on rattlesnakes, and the plant was given the common name of rattlesnake fern. To other observers, the round clusters of sporangia resembled bunches of grapes, and they gave the plant another common name, grapefern. In addition, an old folklore said that wherever this fern grew, ginseng could be found, and one more common name was applied to *B. virginianum*, "indicator" or "sang sign."

The size of the plant is highly variable, and specimens have been reported as small as a few inches to close to three feet tall. In addition, *Botrychiums* differ from other ferns in not having an underground rhizome. Instead, their roots are numerous, fleshy and spreading.

Native Americans found the blade's astringent properties useful for treating open sores, yet in the Himalayas and New Zealand, rattlesnake fern was boiled and eaten instead of being used medicinally.

The mystery and cautious suspicion of snakes have been spread to many of the objects associated with them, and the rattlesnake fern is one such plant. In the plant/medicine association, rattlesnake fern was used for treating snake bites. The Cherokee Indians would boil the roots until the mixture became syrupy, then would apply the salve externally to the wound.

Rattlesnake fern grows well in rich, moist woodlands and wet thickets, though the plant will also grow in dryer conditions. It thrives in shady, subacid soil. Rattlesnake fern makes a pretty addition to a shady garden when planted in slightly acid, rich and loose soil, and is one of the easiest *Botrychiums* to cultivate.

Botrychium dissectum Sprengel

Common grapefern; Dissected grapefern; Lace-frond grapefern

Family: Ophioglossaceae

(Virginia, North Carolina, South Carolina, Georgia)

57. *Botrychium dissectum*/Common grapefern

Common grapefern is another lacy-looking fern and at first glance reminds one of rattlesnake fern. Yet there is an easy way to tell the two apart. For the rattlesnake fern, the fertile portion of the frond is often several inches above the soil with the sterile leaf growing without a stipe (petiole) from the juncture of the two. In the common grapeferns, the fertile and sterile fronds have long stipes, with the juncture of the sterile and fertile portions so close to the ground or in some cases underground that they appear to be two separate plants. In addition, the sterile frond of the common grapefern is long—from 4 to 15½ inches in height.

Like its relative, the leaves of the common grapefern are triangular and variously dissected, but the leaves of this fern are more leathery and turn a copper-brown or bronze in the winter. Leaflets are long and pointed with tiny teeth on the margins. In addition, there is typically an oblong-shaped lobe that appears on the lowest pair of leaflets. In other words, this lobe looks as though it were cut from the broader leaflet or that one leaflet contains two segments. However, this feature only appears on the lowest leaflets on both sides of the rachis, and only on one side of the leaflet's midvein (see illustration). Grapeferns get their common name from the grapelike cluster of sporangia on the fertile frond. Sporangia grow without indusia, are light yellow in color and develop in the fall (August to October). Roots are branching and fleshy and are often 3 inches or more below the soil.

Botrychium dissectum grows well in moist to dry woods, thickets and alluvial plains, but is most difficult to cultivate due to a soil fungi symbiotic in the roots.

Botrychium biternatum (Savatier) Underwood
Southern grapefern
Family: Ophioglossaceae

(Virginia, North Carolina, South Carolina, Georgia)

58. *Botrychium biternatum*/Southern grapefern

Although not as lacy as the preceding grapeferns, *Botrychium biternatum* has the divided leaflets and grape-cluster sporangia characteristic of this family. The specific epithet means "twice divided in threes" and refers to the way the blade is dissected, though fronds are variable and can be divided once in three's, twice in three's or sometimes a combination of the two.

The plant can grow from 7½ to almost 18 inches tall with leathery blades which are triangular in shape and divided into three sections of leaflets. Leaflets are oblong with pointed tips, have finely toothed margins, and are bipinnate at the base. The fertile frond joins the sterile blade a few inches above or sometimes below the soil level, and though the common grapefern has this same characteristic, the differences in the leaf and leaflet dissection help distinguish the two species. Sporangia mature in late summer and fall. In addition, the roots of this fern are thickish and somewhat corky.

Southern grapefern grows in subacid soil in woods, fields, swamps and pinelands. Because this fern is difficult to cultivate, it is not recommended for the home garden.

Botrychium lunarioides (Michaux) Swartz
Winter grapefern; Moonwort; Lunary; Unshoe-the-horse
Family: Ophioglossaceae

(South Carolina, Georgia)

59. *Botrychium lunarioides*/**Moonwort**

Throughout history, the moon has often been associated with mystery, romance and curiosity, and the fern associated with this heavenly body has its own share of lore, magic and superstition. *Botrychium lunarioides* is a fleshy plant, often no more than 4 to 6 inches high. Its sterile blade, triangular in shape and prostrate on the ground, is divided two to three times with half-moon shaped, finely toothed subleaflets. The fertile frond grows alongside the sterile and is topped by a cluster of sporangia from which the name *Botrychium* is derived.

Some early observers saw the shape of a horseshoe in the moonwort's subleaflets. To them this association gave the fern the ability to attract metal. Thus, moonwort had the ability to unlock houses and safes, and if a horse trod on a pasture containing this small fern, the horse would lose his metal shoes. From this ability comes another of the fern's common names, unshoe-the-horse.

The half-moon shape of the plant's subleaflets probably inspired the authors of the Doctrine of Signatures to give mysterious lunar properties to the plant. Early astrologists assigned the moon a cold, moist nature, the color white and the metal silver. Alchemists in the Middle Ages combined magical associations with changing base metals into more valuable ones, and saw in moonwort the ability to change quicksilver (mercury) into the more highly prized silver.

Debates continue as to whether more accidents and crimes are committed during a full moon. Many of us when explaining what seems an excessive amount of irrational behavior will say in jest, "There must be a full moon tonight," and an old North Carolina belief says that if one sees the moon through the branches of a tree, he will go crazy. But the belief of the moon's influence on unusual behavior dates back centuries. The word *lunatic* comes from the Latin word *lunaticus,* meaning moonstruck or epileptic. People thought, too, that the phases of the moon influenced such periodic disorders as sleepwalking and epilepsy by its waxing and waning. To help in these instances, the moonwort fern was sympathetically employed, provided, of course, that it was gathered only by the light of the moon.

While superstitions abound, early practitioners did indeed use the fern in their medicines. According to the seventeenth-century herbalist, Culpepper, the leaves of *Botrychium lunarioides* were boiled in white wine and taken to stop bleeding and vomiting, and the mixture was helpful when applied to bruises and fractures.

Finding the rare, "magic-filled" moonwort fern is difficult. Leaves begin their growth in the fall, with sporangia ripening from January to April, after which time the plant completely dies back. Early winter, then, would seem a better time to begin the hunt. Moonwort prefers the dry, sandy soil of old fields, pastures and open woods, but because of the usually standing grasses, leaf litter, other plants and the fern's diminutive size, *Botrychium lunarioides* is often inconspicuous.

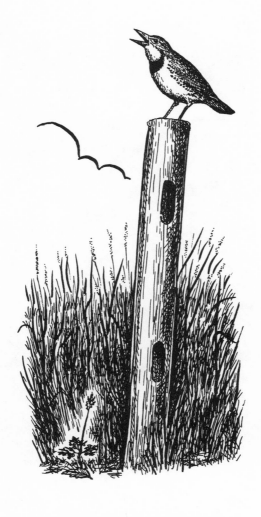

Botrychium lunarioides habitat

Dennstaedtia punctilobula (Michaux) Moore
Hay-scented fern
Family: Dennstaedtiaceae (Pteridaceae)

(Virginia, North Carolina)

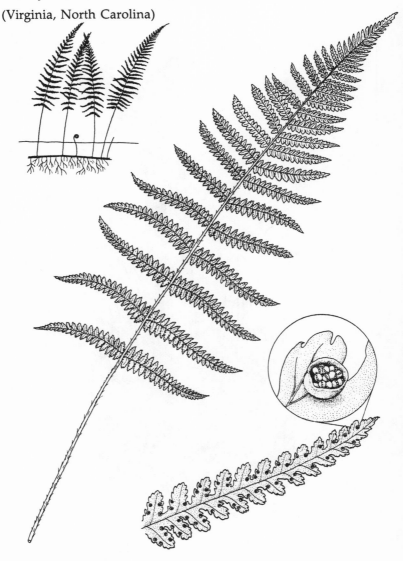

60. *Dennstaedtia punctilobula*/Hay-scented fern

Of all our senses, smell takes the fastest, shortest, most-direct passage to the brain from the nose. Scientists tell us that the emotional centers of our brains developed out of the olfactory lobe. Our sense of smell and our emotions are so intertwined that often a strong smell will trigger a strong emotion. Although today we usually describe, react and respond to the world around us through our sense of vision, there are particular smells that bring back so vivid a memory that if we close our eyes, we can imagine the scene before us.

On walks through the foothills or mountains or along Coastal Plain hillsides, an unmindful brush against the hay-scented fern will send a scent reminiscent of newly mown hay into the air. The smell seems almost out of place with the tall trees all around. Yet those familiar with ferns will recognize the scent and the habitat of *Dennstaedtia punctilobula.*

Full, feathery and delicately arching, the hay-scented fern grows from 1 to 2½ feet tall in short rows. Fronds are lancelike in shape, yellow-green with alternate wavy-margined subleaflets and toothed lobes. The undersides of the leaflets are lined with tiny whitish hairs topped by minute glands which produce the "hay-scent" when bruised.

The fertile fronds have distinctive cuplike indusia along the leaflet's margins. Sporangia fill these tiny "cups" and mature in the late summer and fall.

Medicinally, the Cherokee Indians made a decoction from the fern and used the tea for chills, while other tribes used the nodules at the crown of the plant for lung hemorrhages.

Hay-scented fern can be found along wooded hillsides and rocky slopes. It can be cultivated, spreads rapidly and makes a good cover for a slope. The fern grows in sun or shade in most soils, but does best when grown in a woodland mulch.

Dryopteris intermedia (Muhlenberg) A. Gray

Evergreen wood fern; Fancy fern

Family: Dryopteridaceae (Aspidiaceae)

(Virginia)

61. *Dryopteris intermedia*/Evergreen wood fern

Of the wood ferns growing in the Coastal Plain, the fancy fern is the only one that grows in a symmetrical crown. Fiddleheads are densely covered with cinnamon-colored scales with darker centers that can also be found on the stocky rhizome and light-colored stipe. This is a lacy-looking evergreen fern with fronds 1½ to almost 3 feet tall. The dark green blade is sturdy-looking, fuller than its relatives and somewhat triangular in shape with alternate leaflets and toothed subleaflets. The backside of these fronds contain minute glands which often make the fronds feel sticky.

Fertile fronds have small, round sori covered with horseshoe-shaped indusia found particularly along the midribs. The indusia are also covered with these tiny, clear glands.

Though fairly common in the Northeast and Virginia, *Dryopteris intermedia* is typically found in the mountainous regions of the Carolinas and Georgia. Fancy fern occupies rich, woodland soils, including those of swamps and rocky places. It can be cultivated in a similar garden habitat in moist soil, full shade or partial sun and makes a fine backdrop against large boulders. This fern is often collected and used by florists.

Lygodium japonicum (Thunberg) Swartz
Japanese climbing fern
Family: Schizaeaceae

(South Carolina, Georgia)

62. *Lygodium japonicum*/**Japanese climbing fern**

Coming across this fern as it is twined among tree branches is a surprising experience. The tiny, delicate leaflets at first glance do not appear very fernish, and compared to other vines, the plant's delicate nature seems terribly out of place.

The dark wiry stipes arise from a creeping rhizome and twine, rather than climb, around other plants. The fern grows from 2 to close to 20 feet long with alternate leaflets and variable, variously cut subleaflets. Generally, however, the sterile subleaflets are somewhat triangular in shape and occupy the lower portion of the plant. The fertile subleaflets, also highly variable, are found on the upper part of the plant. Two rows of roundish-oblong sori line the fingerlike tips of the fertile subleaflets making them appear smaller and more constricted than the sterile.

Japanese climbing fern is a plant native to Asia and has escaped from cultivation. Though not overly common, the plant can be found in moist woods, riverbanks and ditch edges. More often, *Lygodium japonicum* is grown in greenhouses, Southern gardens and as a potted houseplant.

Pteridium aquilinum (Linnaeus) Kuhn

Bracken; Eagle fern

Family: Dennstaedtiaceae (Pteridaceae)

(Virginia, North Carolina, South Carolina, Georgia)

63. *Pteridium aquilinum*/Bracken

Often sheltered by towering pines and favored by periodic forest floor burnings, bracken pokes its trichome-covered head through the charred soil early each spring. Against the blackened earth, the tightly coiled fiddleheads create a silver-green, polka-dot effect which later turns into waves of green as the fronds expand and the season progresses.

Bracken is one of the most common ferns found throughout the world. It has an underground rhizome that occasionally grows up to 10 feet deep. This deeply planted structure protects the plant from prescribed or wildfire burnings, drought and cold, and it functions in the non-sexual reproduction process as well as in the storage of food for the production of new fronds each spring. With its aggressive tendency, the rhizomes can grow up to 50 feet per year.

The coarse fronds are rather large and can reach a height of 3 feet. They are triangular in shape with the lower leaflets nearly opposite on the rachis and dissected, and the upper leaflets are more egg-shaped, less divided becoming almost entire as the leaflets approach the apex. Leaflet dissection is variable, but the overall look of the frond is captured in the meaning of the name, *pteridium*—feathery and lacy. Sori are found along the margins of the leaflets, with the edges forming false indusia as they curl over the developing sporangia. New fronds are covered with silver-gray trichomes, and though the fiddleheads first emerge in the circinate pattern of most ferns, as the frond matures it completes the unfurling process by expanding in three prong-like sections.

The word *aquilinum* means eagle, and early botanists commonly called the plant eagle fern. This title was probably suggested by the pronged, clawlike growth pattern of the crozier or the eagle-wing resemblance of the frond. Some people believed they saw a "spread-eagle" in a cross section of the stipe, so the name may have been inspired by the arrangement of the vascular bundles. Nonetheless, the reference to eagles seems to have stuck with the plant since 1753 when Linnaeus first named the fern.

Because of bracken's widespread distribution, it was used extensively throughout the world. It has been used as a vermifuge, diuretic, astringent and purgative, and the Cherokee Indians used the plant as a tonic, antiseptic and antiemetic. In Europe a tea made from the roots was taken to reduce swelling and hardness of the spleen. When oil was added to the tea decoction, the blend was applied externally as an ointment for flesh wounds. The powdered roots were used to dry up malignant moisture in ulcers in the belief that this remedy helped heal the sores faster. In addition, the smoke from burning bracken fronds was reputed to drive away gnats, snakes and other such "pests."

Many wild food enthusiasts herald bracken as one of the best-tasting spring vegetables. Recipes range from salads and soups to vegetable dishes and stew-pot additions. The Japanese used the fiddleheads extensively in their food preparations, and the North American Indians roasted the starch-filled rhizomes and pounded them into a flour for bread. In Norway and Siberia the fiddleheads were used as a malt in the brewing of a beer-like beverage. However, recent studies have shown that bracken contains thiaminase, which destroys thiamine and results in vitamin B_1 deficiency. In addition, severe poisoning of cattle and horses has resulted when they browse on the fern's expanded fronds. Studies have also found the fern to be carcinogenic, and therefore bracken should be avoided as a foodstuff.

However, its other economic uses are still of value. The astringent chemicals found in the rhizome makes this a suitable plant for tanning animal skins, and it was once used as a dressing in the preparation of kid and chamois leather. In addition, various parts of the fern have been used with assorted mordants to produce different dye colors. The colonists in Plymouth made an olive green dye from the fern tops mordanted with alum and coppers. In the Scottish Highlands bracken rhizomes and chrome were used to produce the dark yellow of some tartans. The boiled roots, which turn black, formed the black pattern materials among the Washo, Mono and Yokut Indians. Untreated, the rhizome produced the brown pattern used in weaving by many other North American Indian groups.

Before the introduction of soda from sea salt and other sources, the ashes of bracken, containing large amounts of alkali, were used for glassmaking. As the ashes also contain quantities of potash (20 percent of the green fronds and stems are potash) they were used as a substitute for making soap—heated hot enough to make lye or boiled with tallow to make a less caustic cleaner. This potash can also be used as a fertilizer for vegetable and flower gardens. It's estimated that to obtain 1 ton of potash, 50 tons of dry fern are needed. However, bracken potash is soluble and should be collected and stored when dry. In this regard, folklore tells us that in the seventeenth century, bracken was purposely set on fire to produce rain—so keep an eye on the sky if you're going to make soap!

Dry bracken fronds have been used as strainers, thatch, packing material for fruit, barn litter and in the garden to protect young plants. In Roman times dried fronds were used as bedding for soldiers. In addition, bracken was used as a high-heat fuel in lime and brick kilns, breweries and bakeries.

In the forest bracken provides a cover for wildlife. Deer, grouse, turkey, rabbits, birds and other species often use the bracken stands as a shelter or as a bed. The bracken borer moth, *Papaipema pterisii*, lays its eggs on the rhizomes of the fern; the larvae will feed on this portion of the plant until maturity. Like the other fern borers, the bracken borer moth is small with a wing span of only 1 to 1¼ inches. It has orange front wings with lilac to brown shading toward the wings' edges, two oval spots which form a white bar, cream-colored to yellowish hind wings, and the moth can usually be spotted from August to September.

The strands of xylem, which conduct water and minerals, and the phloem tissues, responsible for food conduction, can be seen when the stipe is cut crosswise. Many folktales have been given to the arrangement of these vascular bundles. To some people in Scotland, the shape represented the figure of "King Charles in the oak," alluding to the escape of King Charles II from his enemies by hiding in a grove of oak trees. To others the figure

64. *Papaipema pterisii/* **Bracken borer moth**

of the oak tree itself was represented. In Ireland the arrangement is believed to be the letters "G.O.D.," and thus the plant is called "Fern of God." Yet to still other people the bundles form the letter

"C" for Christ, or "X" (chi), the Greek letter for Christos. Such holy symbols gave the bracken magical powers to protect oneself from evil.

Bracken grows well in full sun, sandy soils and thickets, but rarely in rich woodlands. In those forests where floors are periodically burned to encourage wildlife, bracken is the most predominant species of fern.

Pteridium aquilinum **growth pattern**

Thelypteris torresiana (Gaudichaud-Beaupre) Alston
Mariana maiden fern
Family: Thelypteridaceae (Aspidiaceae)

(South Carolina, Georgia)

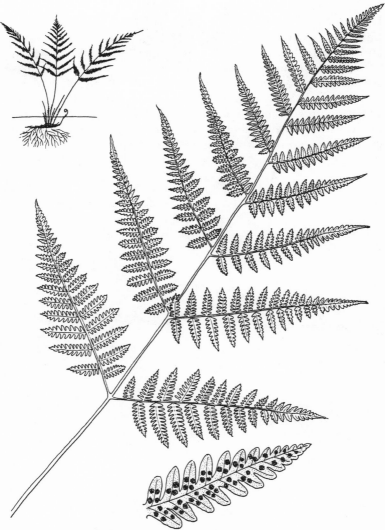

65. *Thelypteris torresiana*/Mariana maiden fern

Arching over the stream's edges, the Mariana maiden fern looks like tall, downy plumes. The fern is rather large, reaching heights of 2 to 4 feet. From a creeping, scaly rhizome, the clustered fronds produce a light-colored stipe with brown scales at its base. The hairy blade is triangular shaped and delicately featherish. Leaflets are alternate and cut further into subleaflets, further cut almost to the midvein with tiny, sharply edged teeth on their margins.

Fertile fronds contain rows of round sori located near the midvein. Though indusia cover the sporangia, the indusia disappear quickly and give the appearance of being absent.

In early times, the growth pattern of plants often suggested to the authors of the Doctrine of Signatures the healing properties of the particular species. For others, the growth pattern often calls to mind images of similar plants or animals. Mariana maiden fern's feathery habit is reminiscent of the beautiful and expensive plumes of the quetzal bird.

The quetzal is vividly colored with scarlet undersides and a bright green head. It lives on insects and fruit and has become the national bird of Guatemala. The male, as for most bird species, is more beautiful than the female and has a long train of shining green tail feathers—often close to 2 feet long. These flowing tail feathers were collected by the middle American Indians to adorn royal and ceremonial objects, and quetzal feathers became a sign of high rank and prestige—a symbol of the ruling rich.

The quetzal bird was also associated with the feathered snake god, Quetzalcoatl, a mythical creature held precious by the Aztec and Toltec. Quetzalcoatl, meaning "precious feather snake" or "green feather snake," was worshipped throughout most of Middle America. This deity was responsible for making fire, the heavens and the great fish, Cipactli, from whom the earth was created. In addition, Quetzalcoatl introduced the calendar, taught agriculture and various aspects of metallurgy. He was kind and opposed human sacrifice and instead, offered bread, incense, flowers and perfume to the gods.

However, we don't have to be rich or sacrifice a magnificent creature to enjoy a similarly beautiful green feather—the graceful fronds of the Mariana maiden fern.

Thelypteris torresiana grows in wet woods and along stream banks. Though only reported from Berkeley county in South Carolina and the Coastal Plain counties in Georgia, experts are watching the fern's appearance in other regions as it spreads from its first reported site in Florida.

Mariana maiden fern can be cultivated in a shady garden in moist soil where its richness can be enjoyed throughout the spring, summer and fall.

Appendix

Counties and cities covered

Virginia

Accomack
Charles City
Essex
Gloucester
Isle of Wight
James City
King and Queen
King George
King William
Lancaster
Matthews

Middlesex
New Kent
Northampton
Northumberland
Prince George
Richmond
Southampton
Surry
Westmoreland
York

City of Chesapeake
City of Hampton
City of Newport News
City of Norfolk
City of Poquoson
City of Portsmouth
City of Suffolk
City of Virginia Beach

Virginia Fall Belt
(counties in both the coastal plain and piedmont)

Arlington
Caroline
Chesterfield
Dinwiddie
Fairfax
Greensville

Hanover
Henrico
Prince William
Spotsylvania
Stafford
Sussex

North Carolina

Beaufort
Bertie

Bladen
Brunswick

Camden
Carteret
Chowan
Columbus
Craven
Cumberland
Currituck
Dare
Duplin
Edgecombe
Gates
Greene
Hertford
Hoke
Hyde
Jones

Lenoir
Martin
New Hanover
Onslow
Pamlico
Pasquotank
Pender
Perquimans
Pitt
Robeson
Sampson
Scotland
Tyrrell
Washington
Wayne

North Carolina Fall Belt

Anson
Halifax
Harnett
Johnston
Lee
Montgomery

Moore
Nash
Northampton
Richmond
Wilson

South Carolina

Allendale
Bamberg
Barnwell
Beaufort
Berkeley
Calhoun
Charleston
Clarendon
Colleton
Darlington
Dillon
Dorchester

Florence
Georgetown
Hampton
Horry
Jasper
Lee
Marion
Marlboro
Orangeburg
Sumter
Williamsburg

South Carolina Fall Belt

Aiken
Chesterfield
Edgefield
Kershaw
Lancaster
Lexington
Richland
Saluda

Georgia

Appling
Atkinson
Bacon
Baker
Ben Hill
Berrien
Bleckley
Brantley
Brooks
Bryan
Bulloch
Burke
Calhoun
Camden
Candler
Charlton
Chatham
Chattahoochee
Clay
Clinch
Coffee
Colquitt
Cook
Crisp
Decatur
Dodge
Dooly
Dougherty
Early
Echols
Effingham
Emanuel
Evans
Glascock
Glynn
Grady
Houston
Irwin
Jeff Davis
Jefferson
Jenkins
Johnson
Lanier
Laurens
Lee
Liberty
Long
Lowndes
Macon
Marion
McIntosh
Miller
Mitchell
Montgomery
Peach
Pierce
Pulaski
Quitman
Randolph
Richmond
Schley
Screven
Seminole
Stewart
Sumter
Tattnall

Telfair

Terrell

Thomas

Tift

Toombs

Treutlen

Turner

Twiggs

Ware

Washington

Wayne

Webster

Wheeler

Wilcox

Wilkinson

Worth

Georgia Fall Belt

Baldwin

Bibb

Columbia

Crawford

Hancock

Jones

McDuffie

Muscogee

Talbot

Taylor

Warren

Glossary

acidic: The result of the chemical nature of the soil as resulting from the type of rock and decomposition of vegetation that form(ed) the soil. An acid soil has a pH below 7 on a pH scale of 0-14 (7 being neutral).

alluvial plain: The land found along river beds or edges that has had soil deposited on it from flooding. Soil usually consists of clay or sand.

alternate: Growth that occurs at different points along an axis, as in "alternate" leaflets.

alternation of generations: The two very different reproductive forms of a fern's life cycle: one, the sexual, *gametophyte* or *prothallium* form; the other, the asexual or *sporophyte* form.

antheridia: The male reproductive structures found on the prothallium. Produces flagellated sperm.

apex: The tip.

archegonia: The female reproductive structures found on the prothallium. Produces egg cell.

authority: The name that follows the scientific name and represents the person(s) who first named and described the plant.

base: The lowest part or bottom.

bipinnate: Cut three times; the further division of a pinnate leaflet.

blade: The green, leafy tissue of a fern.

calcareous: Containing a large amount of lime.

circumneutral: Soil that is very slightly acid or alkaline.

creeping: As in "creeping rhizome"—describes rhizomes that are renewed each year at one end while a portion of the opposite end dies off.

crown: Growth that forms a vase-shaped cluster.

crozier: The coiled, young fern leaf.

decoction: Made by extracting the medicinal properties of the plant by boiling it in water.

dissected: Cut into segments.

Doctrine of Signatures: The early theory that combined medicine, astrology, botany and superstition in the belief that nature had given particular shapes to leaves and flowers to help us determine the specific ailment the plant was intended to cure.

entire: Smooth and continuous; margins that are not cut into segments, wavy or toothed.

epiphyte: A plant that grows on another plant for support; it does not derive any food or nutrients from the host plant.

evergreen: Having green leaves throughout the year.

extract: Removal of certain properties of the plant by pressing, distilling or using a solvent (often alcohol or water); results are more volatile than spirits.

fertile: The reproductive stage of a fern's life cycle; i.e., gametophyte.

fiddlehead: The coiled, young fern leaf.

frond: The leaf of the fern consisting of stipe (also called petiole), used for support and water and mineral transfer from the rhizome, roots and leaves; and the blade, the green, leafy part which carries on photosynthesis. Typically, the blade is divided into smaller leaflets. Besides their aesthetic and food producing value, fronds also bear spores that are responsible for the sexual reproduction of the plant.

gametophyte: The prothallium or sexual stage in the life cycle of a fern.

genus: A group of related species. In the nomenclature represents the first part of a scientific name, i.e., *Pteris*.

globular: Round like a ball.

green manure: A crop that is grown to be plowed under while it is still green to benefit and enrich the soil.

habitat: The area in which an organism lives and which includes moisture, soil and other such conditions.

indusia (pl.) indusium (sing.): A flap of tissue which in some species of ferns covers each sorus, and lends protection to the developing spore cases and spores.

infusion: The steeping of the plant material either in cold water or hot water in order to obtain its active properties.

lamina: The leaf blade of a fern.

lance: The shape which is broadest in the middle and which tapers at both the apex and base.

leaflet: A single division of a fern's blade; also called pinna.

linear: Long and narrow, with parallel sides.

lobe: A portion or segment of a leaf or leaflet that is very small in size.

margin: The edges of the blade or leaflet.

midrib: The vein in the center of the leaflet or undivided leaf.

nomenclature: The system of naming plants, animals, rocks or other objects usually consisting of two parts: the generic name and the specific epithet.

oblong: Longer than broad and with more or less parallel sides.

opposite: Across from one another as in "opposite" leaflets.

panacea: A cure-all.

peltate: Attached from the center like an umbrella.

photosynthesis: The plant process that converts light energy from the sun into chemical energy used in the production of carbohydrates and all materials of the plant.

pinna: A single division of a fern's blade; also called leaflet.

pinnate: Like a feather—with the leaflets in two rows along the central axis.

pinnules: A second division of a fern's blade; also called subleaflets.

prothallium: The gametophyte or sexual stage of the fern's life cycle. The prothallium, when mature, resembles a flat, heart-shaped structure without true roots or stems.

purgative: A substance that cleanses by removing undesirable elements or impurities.

rachis: The central part of the fern to which the green leafy tissue of the blade is attached. (The continuation of the stipe.)

rhizoids: Rootlike filaments that help the plant absorb moisture and nutrients from the soil and anchor the prothallium to the soil. Lack vascular tissues.

rhizome: The underground stem of the fern whose function is to anchor the plant, store starch, produce roots, and through non-sexual reproduction, grow new plants.

rootstock: Underground stem.

scaly: Having small, flattish, usually elongate epidermal outgrowths.

sori (pl.) sorus (sing.): The collective term for the clusters of sporangia (or spore cases) in which the dustlike spores develop. "Fruitdots" is a term often used for the sori but is rather misleading since ferns do not bear fruit. Sori will often appear green at first and later turn into dark brown spots.

species: The basic unit of plant. Consists of all similar classifications. Plants that can breed with one another and are different from all other plants and more like one another.

specific epithet: The second part of the scientific name in the nomenclature, i.e., the word *"multifida"* in the scientific name *Pteris multifida.*

spherical: Round, shaped like a ball.

spirits: Solutions of volatile liquids.

sporangia: Also called spore cases; structures that contain the spores. Each resembles a capsulelike container attached to the leaf by a tiny, thin stalk.

spores: Simple, one-celled reproductive units which, upon germination, develop into the prothallium stage of the fern.

sporocarp: A multicellular structure formed by the fusion of the fertile frond's leaf margins in Salviniaceae.

sporophyte: The non-sexual stage in the life cycle of a fern represented by the obvious fern plant that produces spores.

sterile: The non-sexual stage of a fern's life cycle, i.e., sporophyte.

stipe: The petiole or portion of the leaf below the green, leafy tissue called the *blade.* (Note: The portion of the central axis above the stipe from which the leaflets of the blade are attached is called the *rachis.*)

subleaflet: A second division of a fern's blade; also called pinnules.

symbiotic: An intimate relationship between two plants or a plant and animal that is usually mutually beneficial to both.

teeth: Protuberances of the margin that are usually sharply pointed.

tincture: An alcoholic or water extraction of plant substances. Tinctures are more diluted than fluid-extracts, yet more volatile than spirits.

tonic: A stimulating agent that can be used mentally, morally or physically, and is often used to restore strength and tone.

toothed: Describes margins of a leaf or leaflet when they are sharply pointed.

variable: Diverging in size or shape.

volatile: Easily or quickly evaporated.

zygote: The beginning of the sporophyte or non-sexual stage of a fern's life cycle; the fertilized egg.

Bibliography

Abbe, Elfriede. *The Fern Herbal including the Ferns, the Horsetails and the Club Mosses.* New York: Comstock Publishing Associates, 1981.

Banks, William H., Jr. "Ethnobotany of the Cherokee Indians." M.A. diss., University of Tennessee, 1953.

Borror, Donald J. and Richard E. White. *A Field Guide to the Insects of America North of Mexico.* The Peterson Field Guide Series. Boston: Houghton Mifflin Co., 1970.

Bragg, Laura M. "Preliminary List of the Ferns of the Coast Region of South Carolina North of Charleston." *American Fern Journal* 4 (1914): 83–93. Bulletin of the Charleston Museum 10 (Feb. 1914): 17–22.

Brown, Clair A. and Donovan S. Correll. *Ferns and Fern Allies of Louisiana.* Baton Rouge: Louisiana State University Press, 1942.

Clute, Willard Nelson. *Our Ferns: Their Haunts, Habits and Folklore,* 2nd ed. New York: Frederick A. Stokes Co., 1938.

Cobb, Boughton. *A Field Guide to the Ferns and Their Related Families of Northeastern and Central North America.* The Peterson Field Guide Series. Boston: Houghton Mifflin Company, 1963.

Cooper, J. C. *An Illustrated Encyclopedia of Traditional Symbols.* New York: Thames and Hudson, 1979.

Copeland, E. B. "Edible Ferns." *American Fern Journal* 32, no. 4 (Oct.–Dec. 1942): 121–126.

Core, Earl. "Ethnobotany of the Southern Appalachian Aborigines." *Economic Botany* 21 (1967): 199–214.

Culpepper, Nicholas. *Culpepper's Complete Herbal.* [1653]. Reprint. Secaucus, N.J.: Chartwell Books, 1985.

Felger, Richard S. and Mary Beck Moser. "Serri Indian Pharmacopoeia." *Economic Botany* 28 (1974): 395–430.

Fielder, Mildred. *Plant Medicine and Folklore.* New York: Winchester Press, 1975.

Fleisher, Mark S. "The Ethnobotany of the Clallam Indians of Western Washington." *Northwest Anthropological Research Notes* 14, no. 2 (1980): 192–210.

Folkard, Richard, Jr. *Plant Lore—Legends and Lyrics Embracing the Myths, Traditions, Superstitions and Folk-Lore of the Plant Kingdom.* London: Sampson Low, Marston, Searle, and Livington, 1884.

Foster, F. Gordon. *The Gardener's Fern Book.* Princeton: D. Van Nostrand, 1964.

Frankle, Edward. *Ferns: A Natural History.* Brattleboro, Vt.: Stephen Greene Press, 1981.

Frazer, Sir James George. *The Golden Bough: A Study in Magic and Religion.* New York: Macmillan, 1950.

Friend, Rev. Hilderic. *Flowers & Flower Lore.* London: 1884. Reprint. Rockport, Mass.: Para Research, Inc., 1981.

Gerard, John. *The Herbal or General History of Plants* [1633]. Rev. & enl. by Thomas Johnson. New York: Dover Publications, 1975.

Grieve, M. *A Modern Herbal: The Medicinal, Culinary Cosmetic and Economic Properties, Cultivation and Folk-lore of Herbs, Grasses, Fungi, Shrubs & Trees with Their Modern Scientific Uses—In Two Volumes.* New York: Harcourt, Brace & Co., 1931. New York: Dover Publications, 1982.

Hamel, Paul B. and Mary U. Chiltoskey. *Cherokee Plants: Their Uses—A 400 Year History,* (self-published) 1975.

Hamilton, Edith. *Mythology.* The Universal Library, Grosset & Dunlap, 1978.

Hand, Wayland D., ed. *The Frank C. Brown Collection of North Carolina Folklore.* vols. 6, 7. Durham, N.C.: Duke University Press, 1961.

Hedrick, U. P. ed. *Sturtevant's Edible Plants of the World.* Albany, N.Y.: Department of Agriculture's Twenty-seventh *Annual Report,* vol. 2, part 2, 1919. Reprint. New York: Dover Publications, 1972.

Hendrix, Stephen D. "An Evolutionary and Ecological Perspective of The Insect Fauna of Ferns." *The American Naturalist* 115, no. 2 (Feb. 1980): 171–196.

Hudson, Charles. *The Southeastern Indians.* Knoxville, Tenn.: The University of Tennessee Press, 1976.

Hunt, Kenneth W. "Ferns of the Vicinity of Charleston, S.C." Charleston Museum Leaflet no. 17 (Dec. 1942).

Jobes, Gertrude. *Dictionary of Mythology, Folklore and Symbols.* parts 1 and 2. New York: Scarecrow Press, 1962.

Kehoe, Alice Beck. *North American Indians: A Comprehensive Account.* Englewood Cliffs, N.J.: Prentice-Hall, 1981.

Kingsbury, John M. *Poisonous Plants of the United States and Canada.* Englewood Cliffs, N.J.: Prentice-Hall, 1964.

Lasne, Sophie and Andre Pascal Gaultier. *A Dictionary of Superstitions.* Englewood Cliffs, N.J.: Prentice-Hall, 1984.

Latorre, Dolores L. and Felipe A. "Plants used by the Mexican Kickapoo Indians." *Economic Botany* 31 (July–Sept. 1977): 340–357.

Leach, Maria, ed. *Funk & Wagnalls Standard Dictionary of Folklore, Mythology, and Legend.* New York: Harper & Row, 1984.

Lellinger, David B. *A Field Manual of the Ferns and Fern-Allies of the United States and Canada.* Washington, D.C.: Smithsonian Institution Press, 1985.

Lewis, Walter H. and Memory P. F. Elvin-Lewis. *Medical Botany: Plants Affecting Man's Health.* New York: John Wiley & Sons, 1977.

Lloyd, Robert M. "Ethnobotanical Uses of California Pteridophytes by Western American Indians." *Economic Botany* 54, no. 7 (1964): 76–82.

Lovelock, Yann. *The Vegetable Book: An Unnatural History.* New York: St. Martin's Press, 1972.

Lumpkin, Thomas A. and Donald L. Plucknett. "*Azolla*: Botany, Physiology, and Use as a Green Manure." *Economic Botany* 34 (1978): 111–153.

Lust, John B. *The Herb Book.* New York: Benedict Lust, 1974.

Massey, A. B. *Virginia Ferns and Fern Allies.* University of Richmond, Virginia Extension Service Bulletin no. 273, 1969.

Matthews, Velma D. "The Ferns and Fern Allies of South Carolina." *American Fern Journal* 30, no. 3; 31 (July–Sept. 1940; 1941): 73–80, 119–128; 4–12.

May, Lenore Wile. "The Economic Uses and Associated Folklore of Ferns and Fern Allies." *Economic Botany* 44, no. 4 (Oct.–Dec. 1978): 491–528.

Mooney, James. *Myths of the Cherokee and Sacred Formulas of the Cherokees* from the 19th and 7th Annual Reports of the Bureau of American Ethnography 1900. Nashville, Tenn.: Charles and Randy Elder-Booksellers, 1982.

Mooney, James and Frans M. Olbrechts. *The Swimmer Manuscript: Cherokee Sacred Formulas and Medicinal Prescriptions*. Washington, D.C.: Smithsonian Institution Bureau of American Ethnology, Bulletin 99, 1932.

Morton, C. V. "A Shorter Note: The Use of Climbing Fern, Lygodium, in Weaving." *American Fern Journal* 56 (1966): 79–81.

Morton, Julia F. "Principal Wild Food Plants of the United States." *Economic Botany* 17, no. 4 (Oct.–Dec. 1963): 319–330.

————. *Medicinal Plants of Middle America: Bahamas to Yucatan*. Springfield, Ill.: Charles C. Thomas, 1981.

Norton, Helen H. "Evidence for Bracken Fern as a Food for Aboriginal Peoples of Western Washington. *Economic Botany* 33, no. 4. (Oct.–Dec. 1979): 384–396.

Parsons, Frances Theodora. *How to Know the Ferns: A Guide to the Names, Haunts and Habits of Our Common Ferns*. Charles Scribner's Sons, 1899. Reprint. New York: Dover Publications, 1961.

Porcher, Francis P. *Resources of the Southern Fields and Forests, Medical, Economical, and Agricultural*. Reprint. Charleston, S.C., 1863. New York: Arno & The New York Times, 1970.

Porcher, Richard D. *A Field Guide to The Bluff Plantation*. Louisiana: The Kathleen O'Brien Foundation, 1985.

Radford, Albert E., Harry E. Ahles, and C. Ritchie Bell. *Manual of the Vascular Flora of the Carolinas*. Chapel Hill, N.C.: University of North Carolina Press, 1968.

Ridgeway, Robert. *Color Standards and Color Nomenclature*. Washington, D.C., 1912.

Roberts, Edith A. and Julia R. Lawrence. *American Ferns: How to Know, Grow and Use Them*. New York: Macmillan, 1935.

Roberts, Nancy. *Ghosts of the Carolinas*. Charlotte, N.C.: McNally and Loftin, 1983.

Skinner, Charles M. *Myths and Legends of Flowers, Trees, Fruits, and Plants in All Ages and in All Climes*. Philadelphia: J. B. Lippincott Co., 1939.

Smith, Huron H. *Ethnobotany of the Forest Potawatomi Indians.* Bulletin of the Public Museum of the City of Milwaukee, vol. 7, no. 1, May 9, 1933, 1–230.

_____. *Ethnobotany of the Menomini Indians.* Wisconsin: Bulletin of the Public Museum of the City of Milwaukee, vol. 4, no. 1, December 10, 1923, 1–174.

Snyder, Lloyd H., Jr. and James G. Bruce. *Field Guide to the Ferns and Other Pteridophytes of Georgia.* Athens: University of Georgia Press, 1986.

Taylor, Lyda Averill. *Plants Used as Curatives by Certain Southeastern Tribes.* Cambridge, Mass.: Botanical Museum of Harvard University, 1940.

Tenenbaum, Frances. *Gardening with Wildflowers.* New York: Ballantine, 1973.

Turner, Nancy Chapman and Marcus A. M. Bell. "The Ethnobotany of the Coast Salish Indians of Vancouver Island." *Economic Botany* 25 (1971): 63–99.

_____. "The Ethnobotany of the Southern Kwakiutl Indians of British Columbia." *Economic Botany* 27 (July–Sept. 1973): 257–268.

Werth, Charles R., Melanie L. Haskins and Akke Hulburt. "Osmunda cinnamomea forma *frondosa* at Mountain Lake, Virginia." *American Fern Journal* 75, no. 4 (Oct.–Dec. 1985): 128–132.

Wherry, Edgar T. *The Southern Fern Guide: Southeastern and South-Midland United States.* New York: Doubleday, 1964.

Yanovsky, Elias. *Food Plants of the North American Indians.* U.S. Department of Agriculture Miscellaneous Publication no. 237, Washington, D.C., 1936.

Index

References to illustrations are in **boldface** type.